DOMINIC NEGUS
'INTO THE LIGHT'

by Jamie Boyle

Facebook.com/warcrypress
Jamie Boyle (c)

ISBN: 978-1-912543-21-2

DOMINIC NEGUS – INTO THE LIGHT': All rights reserved. No part of this publication may be reproduced or transmitted in any form or by any means, including photocopying and recording, without the written permission of the copyright holder, application for which should be addressed to the publisher via the dealing agent at: warcrypress@roobix.co.uk Such written permission must also be obtained before any part of this publication is stored in a retrieval system of any nature. This book is sold subject to the Standard Terms and Conditions of Sale of New Books and may not be re-sold in the UK below the net price fixed by the Publisher / Agent.

DOMINIC NEGUS – INTO THE LIGHT': Produced by www.wacrypress.co.uk (part of Roobix Ltd: 7491233) on behalf of Jamie Boyle, Northallerton. Copyright © Jamie Boyle 2017. Jamie Boyle has asserted his right as the author of this work in accordance with the Copyright, Designs and Patents Act 1988.

Thanks to Sean Keating 'P4P Photos' for use of the cover image, manipulated for cover art by Gavin Parker UK

Printed and bound in Great Britain by Clays, Elcograf S.p.A

Find out more at: facebook.com/negusintothelight/

I dedicate this book to my Dad Cyril Walter Negus. I wish I could be half the man he was. Also, to my girl Annabella Sadie Negus. The Daughter who has made me into such a better person. Everyday I'm blessed to call you my Daughter x

Chapters

Foreword	1
Author's Introduction	4
Chapter One	11
Chapter Two	17
Chapter Three	30
Chapter Four	37
Chapter Five	42
Chapter Six	49
Chapter Seven	57
Chapter Eight	66
Chapter Nine	75
Chapter Ten	82
Chapter Eleven	88
Chapter Twelve	94
Chapter Thirteen	102
Chapter Fourteen	108
Chapter Fifteen	115

Chapter Sixteen	119
Chapter Seventeen	125
Chapter Eighteen	130
Chapter Nineteen	136
Chapter Twenty	143
Chapter Twenty One	153
Chapter Twenty Two	156
Ben Jones	164
Mike Jackson	169
Micky Theo	172
Iain McCallister	177
Dominic Shepherd	179
Thanks	182
Message from Dominic	184

"Big Dom has been a face on the boxing scene for a long time – amateur, professional, the other circuit, security and trainer. He's also a friend, a man and somebody I can trust with Information".

~ Steve Bunce

Foreword

RICKY HATTON

I met Dominic Negus very early on in my career when I was coming up as just a youngster on the small hall shows. Although, it wasn't only at small hall shows that I would see Dom about as he was always the head of the security when Prince Naseem was topping the bills for Frank Warren.

I've got to know Dom very well over the years and he has become a good friend, even after we had both finished our career's we have remained friends and kept in touch. I even went down to London a few years back with my friend, Chris Bacon, who Dom boxed, for Dom's 40th birthday bash as a surprise, he wasn't expecting us to be there we just turned up.

When Dominic boxed Chris Bacon it was very hard for me to watch considering how much I thought of the pair as they were bashing lumps out of each other.

These days Dominic is often up my gym with the lads that he trains, but I think me and Dominic would have been friends even if we never met through the boxing. Me and Dom have had such a strong bond over the years and when I've seen what he's been through in his life I can relate in many ways because, like myself with the depression, Dominic's had his ups and downs.

Nowadays, it's nice to see Dom doing so well and getting back on top in life.

Dominic wasn't a bad fighter himself at all he was very hard and as tough as they come in boxing believe me.

You just don't meet many harder and tougher men than Dominic Negus. Dominic gave boxing a good go and he has a passion for the sport which is second to none.

As happens with a lot of people who try boxing, once you've laced them gloves on you either take to it or you don't, and Dominic obviously laced the gloves on, took to it and has loved boxing ever since. Even outside of boxing, just in life in general, Dominic is still fighting.

These days Dom's doing well training Boy Jones among others, so it's still very much in his blood and Dominic Negus is a proper fighting man in every sense of the word.

It's well documented that Dominic has also done a bit of fighting outside the ring and he's had a fight with life I suppose. There's not much Dominic Negus hasn't fought really.

When you look at the fella and the size of Dominic and his reputation, I find it flabbergasting, I mean he's a gentle giant but I still wouldn't like to meet him down a dark alley that's a dead cert.

When you chip away at Dominic Negus and all his layers then all you're going to be left with is just a good guy.

My personal message to Dom is good luck and just try to enjoy life. Yes, you've had a few ups and many downs but I'm a firm believer in life experience shaping a person and I've been in the same situation as you Dominic but all that you've been through has made you what you are today. The downside of what I went through when I retired is what has made me the person I am today, so the bad side of life has made you the stronger person you are today Dominic. After all the crap and shit it is now time for you to just concentrate on being happy.

Love ya pal all the best, your friend Rick X

Author's Introduction

It was July 10th, 2002 and I'd just settled down to watch the BBC'S coverage of the next heavyweight hope Audley Harrisons sixth contest.

To be honest I'd never heard of Dominic Negus before then. The first thing that struck me about this Cockney wide boy I was seeing for the first time was how funny and witty he was. Dominic walked to the ring, at The Wembley Arena, with a "Vic Dark is an innocent man" t shirt on in support of his friend, it was plastered all over his shirt and must have severely pissed off the authorities considering it was on national television.

The fight itself was a six rounder and Dominic was well and truly in the fight for the first three rounds. The talking point of the fight was in the fourth when Harrison scored a flash knock down when Dominic took a knee, only for Audley to walk off then walk back and give him a full-on back hand in the face. Well as you can imagine Dominic exploded like a man possessed. Very much like the cartoon character Yosemite Sam when he's chasing Bugs Bunny and you didn't need to be a lip reader to read what was coming out of Dominic's mouth, not to mention a "Glasgakiss" on Audley's canister for good measure. Referee Ian John-Lewis earned his wages that night and immediately marched Dominic to a neutral corner trying to calm him down. To be honest I've seen fighters get disqualified for a lot less, but John-Lewis didn't even take a point off Dominic because he knew full well what a liberty Audley had taken.

That was my first glimpse of Dominic Negus and I was well impressed.

Boxing royalty Mickey Vann told me only a few years ago during a charity night that I held in Redcar in 2014, that boxing needs characters, well here we had one huge boxing personality in this brash young Essex boy.

I thought I'd be following his career over the next few years and looking out for his name in the Boxing News. Well, Dominic Negus was never to step foot in a British boxing ring again because it turned out he failed a drug test straight after the battle at Wembley Arena.

After Dom's fight against Audley he kind of vanished and was lost into the unlicensed boxing scene, which I was never a fan of, even if I was, I really didn't have any way of following his career in that with me being in the North.

I would never really think of the name Dominic Negus again until the back end of 2005 when he starred in a fly on the wall documentary called 'Underworld Britain'. Me and my brother in law must have watched that program half a dozen times over that Christmas. Anyone who remembers that television program will know what I'm talking about because it was really hard hitting! There was a scene in it where Dominic threatens a man who'd been trying to rip his Dad off when he'd been close to death. Then there was the scenes of an emotional Dominic at his beloved father Cyril's funeral.

That documentary was like your modern classic, sort of in the same mould as Paul Sykes At Large where you just can't help but watch it over and over.

In 2007 Dominic released his debut book called 'Out of The Shadows' published by John Blake and I went to

Berwick Hills library to read it (sorry Dom I never bought it, scummy I know) and I read it within days.

Anybody who's read my other books like Lee Duffy, Paul Sykes etc will know I'm extremely fascinated by people in life just like Dominic Negus. I've always found the underdog or the people that are different absolutely intriguing, I mean who wants to be normal? How many books would a gardener or a car salesman sell if they released a book compared to people just like Dominic Negus? It sounds bad I know but, true crime will always sell, and people have found it fascinating since the days of Jack the Ripper and probably long before that too.

After reading 'Out of the Shadows' I suppose the next time I would hear about Dominic would be the year after in 2008 on 'Danny Dyer's Deadliest Men'. Out of the full series Dominic's stood out the most for me.

Then in 2012 I travelled up to Glasgow for the Ricky Burns v Kevin Mitchell world title fight with my son Thomas, when who did I see, but Dominic Negus. That day, Dominic spoke to me about his old boxing career and he gave a lot of attention to my boy also. I came away from that day thinking what a lovely fella Dominic was.

Many years later, in 2016, I started writing books and one of the names that kept cropping up was Dominic's as I had interviewed him for the 'Tales of Pugilism' book that I wrote, which is basically twenty different boxers journeys into the fight game. If I'm honest I couldn't just take on anybody's book even if it would be for a lot of money. I've had people ask me in the past and although they've been a big name and it would sell, I haven't fancied it. It was only on one of the last books I did that Dominic mentioned to me he was considering doing this and would I be interested? Well of course I was, and I arranged to meet

Dominic in the Hilton Hotel in Leeds in May 2018. Dom was up in Leeds as his fighter Mikey Sayki was on the Josh Warrington v Lee Selby undercard.

I'd met Dominic all those years before in Glasgow and I'd spoken to him by phone, so I was quite familiar with him by this time, so when I was waiting in the hotel for him to come out I went to shake his hand, only for him to grab me like a huge bear attacking his prey and he gave me this enormous hug. When Dominic cuddled me, I could hear and feel the bones in my neck and back crack, I kid you not. Of course, Dominic was only being playful like an over excited dog but my first thoughts of him were "Jesus Christ I wouldn't like a stand up on the cobbles with you"!

Some people you meet in life pretend that they're this hard fighter who can look after themselves. Here in front of me, although I never told him, I was thinking by god he would be the real deal in a fight if he decided to snap. He had this aura oozing from him that told you that you would not want to go toe to toe with this guy, even though he was a perfect gentleman to me, my publishers Rob and Steve of Warcry Press and my wife Shirley. Shirley always has been a good judge of character, me I'm useless and I'd probably have invited Peter Sutcliffe home if I'd met him in the pub, but she said immediately how she liked the energy from Dominic.

The next day I went to Dom's hotel again in Leeds and we did the book plan. He told me for this book he wanted it to be different from the usual hard man shite and wanted to finally put out there who the real Dominic Negus is once and for all. To be honest I understood what he was saying. Dominic's been tarred with the same brush for many years as so many other Southern gangster types and today in 2019 he is so far removed from that image.

I went to stay with Dominic for five days at his house in Essex and right away I knew that here was one scary bastard as hard as they come, but deep down he was still a little boy inside just wanting to be loved. I sensed a real sadness about him in the way he was living at that very moment. Not being with Nik, not being able to see Bella on a day to day basis was gutting for him and I could see his daily struggle in abundance. I mean we all want to be loved right?

I came to my own opinion that here was a truly frightening figure if he got the "hump", but also that Dominic Negus is awfully fragile and sensitive for such a huge domineering figure. I sensed complete regret over his boxing career and he knows full well he can't turn back the clock and have that time again. In his words "I well and truly fucked my chance in boxing by being a prat".

I myself have been studying and following boxing since the age of ten, I'm thirty-eight years of age now. In my humble opinion I think Dominic Negus should have gone on to be British/European champion level. Even the voice of boxing, Steve Bunce, has gone on record and said Dom could have been a genuine contender if he'd only applied himself. That's why Dominic will not see his lads make the same mistakes that he made.

Boxing's a funny old game and no disrespect, but when you think of Paul "Silky" Jones, Stuart Hall and Nicky Cook who all went on to become world champions and the likes of Kevin Mitchell and Herol 'Bomber' Graham never, then that's as clear as the day is long that boxing is all about taking your chances at the right time. Dominic carries the burden around daily that he knows he didn't do himself justice in the boxing game.

In the last six months since starting this book I'd like to think that I've gained a better understanding of who the real Dominic Negus is, and you will too when you have read this book. He might look like one big scary fucker and have the reputation to match but to your average Joe public like me and you then he's a big cuddly teddy bear, although I wouldn't like to get caught stealing milk off his doorstep.

If you've heard of any acts of wickedness dished out by Dominic in the last twenty years then I'd guarantee that there has been a genuine reason for it.

These days Dominic is the quiet family man and keeps away from a life that once led him down a terrible path. By his own admission he turned to the dark side like Darth Vader in those Star Wars films he's obsessed about. That's another side of him not many people will know about, Dominic is really quite geekish and is a massive film buff especially on sci-fi films.

There's isn't a more fitting saying than "Don't judge a book by its cover" when it comes to Dominic, he was classed as one of Essex's most notorious sons and certainly looks the part but he is one of the warmest most genuine people I've had the pleasure to meet.

Myself & Mrs Boyle send you our love and all the very best wishes for your future Dominic.

God bless you, your friend Jamie X

"There's so many languages around today and so many people don't understand them, but everyone understands a punch in the mouth"

Chapter 1

It was a miserable dreary evening and I was in a lovely little bar named Blue Mondays in Buchurst Hill. The club was the place to be back in the noughties and some good friends of mine, named Mark Holt and Spencer, owned the joint. Mark and Spencer were both very good people and I feel I have to apologise to them both, as sometimes I behaved appallingly when I was in their club. To be fair to them both I was always promising that I was going to be on my best behaviour, but I tended not to be.

On this particular night I was in the club toilets and it was about a month after I had been done over by some geezers, who I now consider to be, well I won't call them the three wise men but, I think of them more as my three men of the apocalypse who arrived, as a little message from the lord above to tell me to stop pissing about and tow the bloody line! Before they showed up I was running around doing whatever the fuck I wanted to, which wasn't good! So, I'm sat in the cubicle with my trousers down, I wasn't fit to be out really but of course I was putting on a front , I wanted to get the message across that I wasn't out of the game and I still had an arsehole, when I hear some geezers come in and to all you fucking readers who presume I was, I wasn't doing gear, I was just in my own little world, not to mention the fact I was practically one handed as my other hand had had an axe stuck in it recently! I hear a group of maybe 3-4 men in the toilets. I could hear raised voices, lads pushing about and tarting themselves up when all of a sudden something that was said pricked my ears. I heard someone say, "That Negus is in here". Now this lovely bunch of chaps had got my attention because I knew they were talking about me. Then I hear another voice chip in with "Yeah the big cunt got proper served up and the cunt deserved it, he was always bashing someone up, I'm so facking happy about it". Well I'd just about heard enough, so I flushed the toilet and walked out to greet three of the biggest fans I'd ever had, not! Well their faces were a complete picture. The three of them completely shit themselves as I smiled at them without saying a word. Eh eh eh ... I think was their response but I just said, "Don't worry lads you were right, I did deserve what I got!" I wasn't going to go into the ins and outs of it but I told the three they were correct in what they were saying and I patted each and every one of them on the shoulder before wishing them a pleasant evening. Them three geezers in the toilets probably expected me to splatter them across the walls and maybe years ago I would have done but I actually 100% agreed with them.

In this life you can't lie to yourself and I was being such a pain in people's arses in London and around Essex that that had to happen. Just because I could look after myself, didn't give me the right to throw my weight about. For everyone of you reading this book, before them three geezers ran in my gym with axes and hammers, I'd become someone I'd quite despised and didn't want to be. Yes, people know from my first book 'Out of The Shadows' that I was bullied as a child but I'd gone full circle and become the bully myself. This was never something I'd ever anticipated happening but I knew I'd arrived at that horrible place, destination horrible cunt.

People say there's a really thin line between respect and fear well when I became a man, because I was so big and powerful, my biggest weakness was my strength and it was getting me into trouble. For years I was the fat specky kid in glasses getting kicked the shit out of on a daily basis so when I became a boxer I was so eager to prove myself. I know this sounds corny but all I ever wanted to be was loved and the way I was trying to be loved was sorting everyone's problems out before my own. Of course, that backfired on me and at times I was used for other people's dirty work. Look I know I'll never be brain of Britain but I'm far from stupid, but sometimes I had to portray that aggressive image because it acted as a defence mechanism. Of course, it helped being the way I was if I was going to get money out of people because sometimes using the word 'please' never cut the mustard. I used to tell the boys that were working with me to walk around as proud as a Peacock, never flash or arrogant but we deserved to be working in that place as much as the next man. My good friend "B" used to say "you should go in an establishment like Henry VIII not Larry the Lamb. You should always go out on your shield and in times of great difficulty you stand firm!"

I'll never forget boxing Brockley's Kevin Mitchell at cruiserweight for the Southern Area title in Barking. Me and Kevin boxed each other twice but we're really good pals now. In that second fight between us, all I could hear all the way through that contest was "Henry the VIII not Larry the Lamb" over and over. My eardrum got popped in the fifth and when I told my corner men he replied "It's not the fifth round, it's the eighth Dom" no matter which round I asked what it was he always told me the eighth.

I told the story in my first book, as well as the couple of television documentaries, of me being attacked in the gym with weapons. If I could meet the guys who did it today I'd like to thank them and buy them a pint. I did deserve it because of the lifestyle I was living. Being almost murdered turned out to be a great leveller for me and it's meant that now I will spend the rest of my life heading in a better direction.

Now I'm surrounded by positive people and it's so true about your handful of friends. Back in them days I didn't have any friends and was only surrounded by arseholes and cunts. These days I'd rather go picking up dog shit for a living with a smile on my face than go back to my old life.

Over the years I've worked in straight jobs and people have said "ere Dom you're so and so" but I've told them "you're paying me money so I'm doing as I'm told". I would never bite the hand that feeds me and that life albeit a skint one is a better life than ending up dead and the people around me worrying about what the eventual outcome was going to be for me.

Don't get me wrong it would be nice to win the bloody lottery but that's just how life goes, it's meant to be hard but the things I was doing were making it so hard for me, I was getting involved in crap, well not no more. I've played this life with the cards I've been dealt. Now I know it hasn't been the best hand and I've had a few jokers but I'm still here. I think I've pulled it off by being just alive today (laughs).

No man is a failure when he has really good friends and I so believe that. My fighter, Boy (Ben) Jones junior, has met all my friends and he says, "how come all your friends are millionaires Dom and you've got nothing?" The answer I always give him was that I was too busy being a friend!

Many years ago, I was looking at a massive court case and if found guilty it was going to be a long time away for me. I'd only just got with Nik, the mother of my little girl Annabella. Well to tell you the truth I thought I was fucked and I'd be going to live in Pentonville for 15 years. I used to go walking on my own for miles thinking all kind of awful thoughts of what laid ahead of me. I just couldn't see the light for the hills and I was becoming very depressed. The same week the court case was to start I heard that song 'Here Comes the Sun' on the radio three times in around five days and I just knew everything was gonna be ok.

During the court case itself I was ok and the big man upstairs made sure of that. When people ask me "Do you believe in Jesus Dom?" Well the answer to that is yes very much so. When people talk to me about luck well, Dominic Negus has never been lucky in his life, I'd fall in a bucket of tits and come out sucking my thumb, but that court case, well if I could have used all my bits of luck together and used them up in one go it was that, even though I never did it! It all got dropped in the end. So, if ever I had a bit of luck in life then that was it. I firmly believe that that happened because God has better things lined up for me for later on.

Yes, I made a pig's ear of my boxing career but I've had a good life at times and I've seen some things that you'd never believe for just some rough scruffy kid from the East End. These days I tend to keep out of licensed establishments and that's the way I like it.

I'm 48 now and all them young kids going out looking for big names are hunters like you'd see in the Neanderthal days when they'd go bring a big bison down and eat it. I can understand these kids to a certain degree because I grew up looking up to Lenny McLean and your Roy Shaw's. Them two were proper people in my eyes and real fighting men. That kind of man is a dying breed because these days they wouldn't, as Danny Dyer would say "Get their new smutter dirty", the young of today will just stab you or shoot you. There is no loyalty among criminals now.

"Life is 10% what happens to you and 90% how you react to it"

Chapter 2

My old man, Cyril Walter Negus, really loved his boxing. My Dad used to work for the print(journalist) and he'd come in at 3am when usually the big fights of the seventies would be on showing Ali, Foreman, Frazier, Hagler etc... My old man would be walking around the house shadow boxing and getting well into all the big fights and that was my first memories of the fight game back then and my first memories overall really.

One of my real hero's in the fight game as a boy was Leicester's Tony Sibson but in my Dad was my real fucking hero in life, he did a bit of boxing in the Army too.

I don't think I really won my old man's respect until I took up the fight game. My old fella wasn't the kind of geezer who would dish out compliments, when I gave him a hug he'd shake it off and say, "Leave off soppy bollocks"! I know he couldn't shake off how proud he was of me when I won the Southern Area Cruiserweight title because he went to Clapton with my belt in a bag showing every man in the boozer just what his boy had won. He was proud as a Peacock that weekend. Maybe it was because of the way he was brought up but with my old fella being real old school, if I ever showed him love he would hit me, but only ever in a playful manner. My Dad was the best friend I ever had and it was the boxing that really brought us together.

When I was growing up and my Dad could see that I wasn't training properly in the gym he would tell me there's somebody out there fucking even harder than me, my reply would always be, "yeah but I'll be the closest second they'll ever fucking have!"

Me and my Brother were so fucking lucky to have had the parents we were brought up with, I still miss them both greatly now.

It wasn't really until I became about twelve years of age that I thought seriously about giving this boxing game a go. My first thoughts were that I didn't fucking like it, I mean, who wants to be punched in the face at twelve years of age anyway, so I faded away from it. To be quite truthful I was only giving it a go to make my old man happy but my heart wasn't in it, so I fucked it off. That was me and boxing done until I started doing the door work at nineteen years of age.

I first started going to a club, which wasn't really a proper boxing gym but it was good to sharpen my tools up for my forthcoming career. I think it was one of my really good friends who said to me "Dom you're wasted here, you need to go find yourself a real amateur boxing club because you can have a row". By that time I was no longer the tubby kid with glasses. I was knocking fully grown men out not to mention the fact that I was as game as a Honey Badger. I suppose I'd exploded onto the scene if you like and I was just so keen to show people what I was about now and I wanted naughty situations to arise so that I could iron people out and prove myself.

I did go find my first proper boxing club Gotar (formerly known as Garden City ABC in Essex) and I did the amateur thing. I got my London and England vests. I went and fought abroad and boxed in Norway. As an amateur I was half decent but didn't really set anything alight. I won the North East divisions a couple of times and even got to the London semi's but I only ever had one thing on my mind and that was to become a professional fighter. One thing I was realistic about was that I knew how hard it was going to be. Let's face it, if it was going to be easy then everyone would be doing it wouldn't they!

I eventually turned pro at 26, I wasn't your most dedicated fighter let me say. To put it bluntly I ruined whatever natural potential I had by being a prat outside of the ring and that's certainly something I've got to live with. The one thing that I did have in abundance was that I had fight in me. I'd been fighting all my life because of being bullied. It's commonly known that I had a shit time all the way through school so when I became a boxer it brought it out of me. I was the original tubby kid with glasses and I had my dinner money nicked on a regular basis for other kid's entertainment. I usually wouldn't eat food I'd get a knuckle sandwich for dinner. I suppose mentally this made me tougher for the pro game and as a pro I boxed for the BBBofC Southern Area and WBU Intercontinental titles.

In my first book I touched on the whole of my boxing career so I'm not going to cover old ground. People know I fought Audley Harrison and how I reacted by head butting him when he hit me when I was down so that's nothing new. Of course, what I've got to hold my hands up about is that if I'd have beaten Audley I wouldn't have deserved it. The reason for that being that I cheated and took steroids. It didn't take much working out as soon as I took my top off at the weigh in because I looked like Arnold fucking Schwarzenegger. As soon as Audley and his manager Colin McMillan saw me they were like two little girls complaining. Audley actually shit himself and paid for my piss test with his own money. The reality of what went on is that I effectively shot myself in both feet because whereas normally I was used to boxing at Cruiserweight 13st 8lbs carrying all the new weight of being almost 17st was like trying to swim with concrete strapped to me. I looked like an absolute monster and I was well and truly ripped up but I wouldn't have deserved to win. It would have been so bad if I'd have nicked the decision so thank god I never.

It's because of things like that and because I've lived through it that I won't even let my fighters, who I'm in charge of, drink energy drinks, it all comes out in the wash eventually as it did for me with Audley Harrison and that cost me my professional licence for life.

My boys, Boy (Ben) Jones Junior and Mikey Sakyi, probably get scrutinised that bit more closely because of the things I got up to as a fighter. So, we make sure we double check everything and don't take any chances, they're 100% clean. Bens 22 now and he's only just found out what beer tastes like. Mikey doesn't drink at all. I've told them both that if they want to drink then they can have a drink with me and not behind my back. I do have good banter with Ben and Mikey and I'm lucky to have them two boys.

If I'd have got on the scales versus Audley with my top and tracksuit bottoms on he wouldn't have known for another 36 hours. The only person I have to blame for that is me.

I took on Audley Harrison in July 2002 and really that was the fight I was best known for regarding my boxing career. I'd already been offered the Audley fight before, but I was suffering from stomach pain. When I took the Harrison fight, I wasn't given a great deal of notice, but it was enough to pack a load of weight on. In my preparation for the fight I thought I was going to beat him. Talking to a few of my friends beforehand, the conclusion they came to was Audley was gonna steam roll me because I was only weighing 14st 8lbs and he was around 17st plus. I'm gonna be honest although it's embarrassing to say this, I went on a course of juice (steroids). Up until then steroids were never my thing because I was a fighter but in about two weeks, oh my god! Everything was so different. I was covered in lumps and bumps and I was throwing the weights around with ease. It was an amazing transformation. I know that the reason I've got too much weight on today is because I took steroids, even my doctors have told me that themselves. The Doctor told me taking the juice has blown me up now. He told me all the years of me boiling down to 13st 8lbs and then taking the juice has fucked me well and truly now. I was told only now does my body realise just how much it was starved and of course I'm a big fella being over 6ft 2.

All the people over the years saying, "Ooh that Fraudley Harrison was shit". Well I'm telling you now, that geezer was not shit! You don't get Olympic gold medals if you're shit. A big good un will always beat a good little one and when I boxed him what struck me was that he had tremendous hand speed for such a big guy. Also, Audley's footwork. He hit me with that big left hook of his right down the middle and my head was looking up at the ceiling, I had a Tefal head. Of course, the talking point in the fight was in the fourth round where I nutted him. If you watch the fight again carefully you see he caught me with a decent shot and I went down. Then as Audley walks away he walks back and hits me as hard as he could in the side of the head when I was down and that's when I got the hump. I jumped up and my attitude was you want to fuck about with me I can fuck about with you and I nutted him. The referee that night was Ian John Lewis and he grabbed hold of me, marched me to the corner and calmed me down. I'd say the fight changed then and he went on to beat me 55-59. I was the first one who gave Audley a proper fight, I brought him into the trenches a little bit.

After the fight, what really fucked me off was when I took my Dad in the dressing rooms and Audley blanked us both. Normally, after a fight, what happens is that it all gets left in the ring, you have a pint and a laugh about punching each other's face in but not Audley. That's why I've always had the needle with him for the last 17 plus years. I know he probably had the hump with me because I stuck the nut on him but like I said the fight was over. Well what's your problem Audley? You're the one who had your hand raised in battle!

After the Audley fight that is when I suppose I lost it and turned to the dark side if you like. If people looked at me funny and it was my time of the month I was knocking them out. I didn't care if you were Bruce Lee or Jackie Chan, if I hit you on the chin you were going for a kip and it was around that point in my life when I hated myself the most. I knew I was doing it wrong but I had nobody to tell me I was being a complete prat!

Of course, after the Audley Harrison fight in the summer of 2002 the British Board of Control wouldn't touch me and that was my career well and truly fucked. My mind was all over the place and I fucked off abroad to Tenerife for a good while. When I came back to Britain I still wanted to fight but the only people who would touch me was the unlicensed boxing world. Now beggars can't be choosers so an old dog like me wasn't going to learn new tricks by that point. I still needed to fight and get it all out of my system, so I had 37 unlicensed fights. I won 34 only losing to Mike Tyson's conqueror Danny Williams, Chris Bacon and Karl Barwise. I managed to revenge the loss to Barwise as the second fight didn't last one round, I utterly annihilated the geezer. My loss to Chris Bacon was no disgrace, and I'd just like to go on record now and say Chrispy Bacon is the toughest hardest man I've ever had the pleasure to share a ring with. Today I'm proud to say I can call him a friend. Of course, everyone knows that Danny Williams is the Brixton Bomber and he had one last dance with me, everyone knows how big that fucker is and it was a true honour for me afterwards when he told me I hit him as hard as Tyson did. Danny beat me good and proper, but I have big respect for Danny because I went out and stuck it right on him. That night the bigger and better man won but I'll always love Danny Williams.

I know I should have done so much better than I did under the Queensbury rules but as I said earlier, I got too involved with other things. I basically took my eye off the radar and I became more interested in earning money outside of the ring when I fucking shouldn't have been. Now it's too late and I can't get that time back, I blew my time when I was in my prime and it hurts me today to say that but it's the truth. I thought I was being big, cool and tough when in the cold light of day I was too busy being a cunt! I tell my lads Mikey and Ben that often to warn them of the dangers. I was a cunt, but I was a good cunt not a shit cunt.

At times it kills me to think I let my boxing career go the way it did, a million percent. I've sparred Lennox Lewis, alright Lennox could have beaten the fuck out of me if he'd wanted and most probably won't even remember having a move around with me, but I wouldn't have been put in there in the first place if I never had anything about me. Another top name I was used for sparring for was the American Montell Griffin before he went and boxed Dariusz Michalczewski for the world title. Daruisz's team fucked me off after two rounds saying I was too mad. Dean Powell (god rest him) had arranged it, but they fucked me off and paid me my money after two saying "you're obviously mad mate we don't need that kind of sparring". I was on him like a fucking dog and absolutely smashed him that day in sparring. I was in the gym constantly at the time in 1999.

Myself I think I was good enough to have become world champion, but I fucked it all up because I didn't live for boxing and now at 48 it eats me like a cancer. Someday I scream at my boys, "DO AS I FUCKING TELL YOU", then they'll say "yeah but Dom you didn't as a fighter blah blah blah"... In one respect boxing has saved my life and it's been good because of all the people I've met along the way, I don't think I have that many enemies and certainly not from boxing. The one thing I hope this book does achieve is that I hope it gets me to sit down with Audley Harrison and have a cup of coffee with him, that's the one thing I would love to do. It totally gutted my Dad that after the fight the champ shunned us. I'm not even sure Audley is aware I had my Dad there, he just told his team that he didn't want to see me and that's why I've held the hostility towards Audley for so many years. Maybe to him I was just about twenty-four minutes at Wembley Conference Centre but to me he was a lot more than that and I'd like to find out how life's been treating him and make him aware that I had my old man there that night in his wheelchair when he shunned us because I don't think he's even aware. I'd like to hear that from his mouth.

If you're talking about my hero's in life well look no further than my old Dad. He was the straightest person I've ever met, and he worked every day of his life and that was only for Mum, me and my Brother. Even when my Mum and Dad weren't together she was looked after until the day he died. That's what my Dad was all about so, if I can be half the man in life my old Dad was I'll be doing well.

What I know now I wish I knew then and I'll drum that into my lads. There's a lad in our gym named Ginger Lyle and he's going pro soon. Now he's never going to become world champion but when he's in my gym he gets the gym's attention as much as Boy Jones Junior does. It's who learns the most that counts! Boxing's not a sport to piss about with let me tell you from first hand experiences. I was a good fighter, but I didn't reach half my potential being that I was a knob. Don't get me wrong I trained like a motherfucker, I used to love my training and would often even train on my own when I was away from training. Look at me now I'm a bit of a lump but back in the day I could do 15-20 mile running easy but I wouldn't take on board what I was being told.

Now my old trainer was a lovely old gent named Lenny Butcher but one of my regrets, especially after winning the Southern Area Title at Cruiserweight, was not changing trainers. What I was finding after being on the pads with Lenny after 15 years was nothing changed and Lenny was mainly just amateur. In boxing you've got to evolve, you've got to adapt and you pick up different things. With old Lenny I was never picking up anything new and that meant I was never going to get better under his same old guidance.

These days I take my boys to Ricky Hatton's gym up in Manchester I've taken them up to Joe Gallagher's gym also and I feel so privileged to learn from them special coaches. It's nice learning different things from others and sometimes I get in awe of people. I never get in awe in Ricky Hatton's company because Ricky's Ricky but I know young Ben Jones has. One-time Ricky Hatton took Ben on the pads and he's asked him to loosen up and I could see from a mile off what the problem was, so I popped in and said, "Hang on a minute Rick, you're like his fucking idol" (laughs) The kid Ben was like OMG but then of course Ricky knew it and it was all sorted. When we've been to Joe Gallagher's gym that's been an awesome experience and we've all had pictures of Joe and the lads in the gym such as Anthony Crolla, The Smith brothers and Scotty Cardle. Jimmy and Mark Tibbs have been the same, very nice to us and my boys have learnt a lot. Jimmy Tibbs is old school and also Alan Smith who has had us over to his place and he's one of the best trainers out there and a well of knowledge, not just for my boys but for me as well. Ben Jones has sparred Joe Cordina and let me tell you that's a fighter who's going to be a world champion. For my lad Ben he was lucky enough to share the ring with him doing the rounds he has at an early stage. I'm always on the phone trying to get my boys the best sparring available because I know what it's like being in that ring getting punched in the face for a living when you're having a bad day. Sometimes you think you can't be arsed doing it, so you cut a corner and fuck the run off. It's alright for the promoters because it's not them getting in there.

Sometimes I get nervous when I'm working the corners with my boys because I don't want them getting hurt because I know just how easy it is to get hurt in this game. As far as boxing goes I never really got hurt. Yes, I got hit on the chin or got wobbled and thought "FUCK THAT HURT" but never nothing serious, although I do have a funny eye and have slight double vision in one of my eyes, I also suffer headaches but that's part of the parcel of boxing ain't it!

My style of fighting was always going to be quite hazardous to the health anyways but I wouldn't train someone to fight like I did. I suppose I didn't do too bad and I kept my good looks. My two lads Mikey and Ben, don't get me wrong, can have a fight but I want them to get on their bikes and use the ring. I've been involved in fights where people have got hurt and it does affect you because you know it could easily have been you.

Boxing these days means still a hell of a lot to me. I don't really sit in and watch it like I used to because I'm at the gym everyday with the boys making my living, it can get tedious.

I make a living from boxing these days and I just manage to get by, but it's a clean honest living and I'm only trying to do the best I can for my boys and for myself away from crime. Even if Ben and Mikey fucked off to Adam Booth tomorrow, I'd have to go get a proper job, maybe in security or something. I would never go back to the skulduggery days of the things I've been up to in the past. I have no heart for it and I couldn't cope with the prison sentences that that life brings. Even when I was "at it" I didn't think I was a horrible person, I just had such a reputation that brought that kind of work and the money that that bad life brings.

Everything for me and my extra activities changed after the Audley Harrison fight because the law were far more aware and interested in me and I got too big for my own boots. Sometimes, at the time when I was in my hay day of boxing, I would get a call and I'd be off. I would get a call to go get some big bucks in and the reason I was good at that job was because I took them personally. My close friend used to say "Dom you can't think like that it's just work" but I would never think like that and I wouldn't let it go. I know people go around and say "ooh that Negus is a right horrible cunt" because of the things I used to get up to. It's going to take me maybe for the rest of my life to shake off that tag. Oh my god I got myself a reputation, but I would never walk in places where people spoke to me and I was like "SHUT UP YOU CUNT" and if I did then it's been me messing about with my mates. The one thing in life that I don't want to do is to intimidate anyone anymore. I'll leave that to the youngsters. I've now changed for the better.

Boxing these days is still a big part of my life massively because of the two lads I coach but it's also more than that, it's a way of life. Boxing brought me discipline when I needed it most. It's not always the nicest people you meet in boxing though. All the handshaking at the press conferences isn't worth a wank and you've got to have your blinkers on. I'm known as a very loyal person. I've always been straight and I want people to be straight with me, but you don't always get that in the "hurt business" which is what boxing is.

I don't live like a king, but I suppose that being involved with my fighters means that still, to this day, it provides me with a living. My Mum and Dad are gone now and I have nothing to do with my Brother so my focus in life is Annabella and boxing. My two rising stars are Boy (Ben) Jones Junior 18-2-1 with 8 KO'S and Mikey Sakyi 7-2 with 3 KO'S. Them two little fuckers have no idea just how much they keep me alive. Ben in particular is a future star and he'll be in the mix for titles very soon. If you want to see what the pair of them are about then YouTube them.

Today we're in the 21st century and everything is social media. The reason I have to use Dominic Anthony Negus is because there's some lunatic out there who has been pretending to be me for the last six years. There's nothing as queer as folk Oscar Wilde once said.

"I was so eager to please people, basically so that they'd like me. It was nice to go in the pub and everybody slap me on the back and say, "good man, Dom", but I know now that they were just trying to keep me sweet and that behind my back they were all saying "he's a fucking nutter"

Chapter 3

Out of the Shadows was my first book which was released in January 2007. I don't think that would have ever come about if it wasn't for the Audley Harrison fight because until that point I was unheard of more or less. After the Audley fight I became more well-known, even to the average Joe public for various things in the papers for at least six months after that fight. To be honest that Audley Harrison fight boosted me right into the limelight when I could have done without it. If you think about it, I was a debt collector for a living and maybe a bit of back up for hire, I didn't really need the fame that fight brought upon me. After the fight with Audley at Wembley Arena everything changed for me for the worse work wise.

Everybody knows the Essex Boys story and what they were up to and I know some of the papers were tarring me with the same brush as that mob which was very unfair not to mention untrue. I know that's the reason Danny Dyer and his film crew came after me but of course, a lot of my very good friends were from that life such as Vic Dark. When I boxed Audley I wore a T-shirt which said on the front 'Vic Dark is an innocent man' which I know pissed off the BBBofC big time.

Vic had his book out and then there was a load of football casuals/hard man books coming out all over the place that were published by John Blakes. I considered John Blakes to be the people to go to at that time and I'd been asked by Ivan Sage who used to do all my boxing and amateur articles anyway for the Brentford Gazette so, it just felt right when he asked me if he could write my book on behalf of John Blakes.

At that time, I was being mentioned a hell of a lot in other people's books, so I thought why not do my own if that's what people want to read, so that's how that all came about with Out of The Shadows. That book in itself, if anybody hasn't read it, is about one bullied schoolboy who was kicked the shit out of frequently. When he hit his late teens he got involved in door work in some of the roughest shitholes in and around London/Essex, fell into the ancient art of pugilism and then he began to look after himself and gained a huge reputation to go with it.

I became very well known to people in and around London for my security work also, guarding the top fighters in the big fights. Some of my hardest fights have been pulling two top fighters apart at the weigh-ins. If you think these boys have both been in 12-week camps, haven't eaten what they wanted to or had been able to have sex in that time and when they come face to face with each other then that's when I earn my money.

Away from the boxing and back in the day before the S.I.A licenses came in, if someone was cheeky and put it on you then you could give them a slap back. At that time in my job if someone tried to slap me I could slap back a little bit harder than most people and that's the way it went.

When I realised that me and British boxing were going to be no longer acquainted that's when I really turned to the dark side, just like Darth Vader says in Star Wars and there was nothing I wouldn't fucking do. I was collecting money for people, going on meets and just being a general mercenary basically. I wanted to be the baddest man in the whole of London and for a spell I think I was. At times I was told to go pick huge amounts of money up and take it from A to B and I never asked questions. To be honest I never even opened it, but I knew it was a lot of cash just by the feel of it.

One particular day I went to pick a bag up from Euston Station and there must have been £300,000 in there. At times I was doing shit like that when I was still a kid and here's me handing over a bag like that for £50 but that's what it was all about and if them bags never got to the rightful owner then people would go missing. I've got to say I was seen more as a backup man then a delivery boy. I was known as a person you could take along when maybe a Mr Big was needed to go for a very important meet. When I look back at situations like that it's frightening because even though that is so my old life, I know I was a very silly boy getting involved in the shit I got attached to.

Even today I can get asked to get involved in people's crap even though I'm as straight as Mary Poppins. The best ones are when people try to do it on the sneak and approach me sideways as I call it. How it happens is someone usually comes up to me and says, "you know so and so?" Of course, I do but I just say, "NO I don't know who you're on about!"Then its "yeah of course you do" but I always cut them dead. Sometimes people have rang me up asking me to put it on some geezer I don't even know and when I've replied, "well what's in it for me?" they've been like "Erm…"

I've found out so many fucking times to my pain and discomfort, there ain't no free lunches in this world anymore and if they want me to beat people up then these are people I don't want to be involved with these days.

Since my daughter, who is my whole world, came along on the 6th of September 2004, I've basically kept away from everything. Yes, I got my arse smacked in the gym that day by them three fellas but that was the wakeup call from the Lord above. These days I can go to bed and not worry about someone knocking on the door. Of course, me living that life for as long as I did has it's repercussions, it branded me with paranoia which isn't great. Just because I've changed doesn't mean my old enemies have changed but that's the sad reality and I'm very well aware of that. It could even be another four years down the line when someone might think, "Do you remember that big cunt Negus? Let's go find him" then they find me and they're on my doorstep with a shooter! These days I prefer to keep myself out of the way and I try not to get involved in anyone's crap anymore.

Overall, with my debut book 'Out of The Shadows' I was extremely pleased with it. It gave me a great feeling when people came up and told me they could relate to certain scenarios. If I'm going to be self-critical then my biggest problem with that book was that I didn't publicise it enough. Even now, over ten years later, people are coming up to me saying "Dom I didn't even know you had a book out ya plum"! Well hopefully I won't make the same mistake with this one (laughs).

Obviously you're reading this book now, but I want you to please believe me that I'm not trying to play the big hard man, that's all done and dusted, I'm 48 now. I'm not trying to ruffle people's feathers because I know where I went wrong! What I'm trying to say is that if I can save just one up and coming young lad from going down the path I chose then this book will have been worth it. The harsh reality is that I know from first-hand experience just how fucking shitty life can be. There will never be any contentment or happiness in trying to be the next Dominic Negus. Unless you're on a bender every night getting pissed and sniffing gear with a different woman and you're permanently down. That life is a very lonely life let me tell you. When I was playing jack the lad being a silly bollocks I would wake up every fucking morning and look in the mirror in disgust and say to myself, "WHAT WAS ALL THAT ABOUT, WHY HAVE I DONE THAT?" I wanted to be just happy but I didn't know the way to go about it, I was just a little boy trapped in a 6f 2 man's body but I hated myself and was in constant pain. Sometimes I thought the only way to be loved was to go and beat people up so that it pleased them. I had it so horribly wrong indeed.

Since the book came out I've lost my Mum, Dad had gone already and life has become very awkward for me. Sometimes I just take it on a day to day basis and see how this bloody life pans out. I think all of us on this planet are doing just that.

As I've already said, I accumulated a huge rep for myself and when you have a reputation there's always the "young uns" who want to try you out. There was a place in Essex called The Station which was a right shithole but on every single occasion that I worked that door some fucker wanted a do with me. One night I was working the door therewith my pal big John when a firm came in looking for me and there wasn't even a reason for that other than I had a rep, fucking madness. In situations like that when it was put on me there was no use folding like a deck chair because it's not going to help matters. Neither is it going to help your rep so you've got to front it out. Now this might shock some people but I didn't like doing that job because if you can imagine feeling shit, you then can't say to people in the bar "do you mind not kicking off tonight please fella's because I'm full of the flu". In that type of life you become lost and you learn to fight in the blink of an eye, second nature.

You become so lost to your true self and that happened to me big time. I didn't really want to fight at times then there was times when I was fighting three times a night and I was happy as a pig in shit especially when I was doing the doors out there in Tenerife. At times on the doors I was like an actor and I'd think, who am I going to be today? Am I gonna be a goodie or a baddie, that was the mental shit that would run through my head and it fucked me up for a time. Maybe a psychologist would know more about it than me but with me coming from being a bullied child to being able to fight, I didn't want to turn into that person, but being that person got me respect.

They say there's a thin line between love and hate, but I'd say it was the same between respect and fear. I know years ago when I would walk into places and people would think that's that big horrible cunt Negus over there I better not give him a sideways glance, that's respect but it's the wrong kind of respect in my opinion. Now when I walk into a place today with my daughter Bella and people come up to me, smile and say, "How the bloody hell are you Dom"? that's also respect but the good kind.

Bella really changed my outlook on everything in life. I could look at someone who's took a liberty with someone I love and I think right, I could really punch his fucking head in but then for a split second I would think, I wonder if that geezers having a bad day? Maybe he's just found out his old woman's cheating on him? Maybe he's just been told he's got cancer, whereas before it would have just been BANG goodnight sweet prince and ask questions at his hospital bedside. I like to think things through now before I react.

"My biggest weakness was my physical strength. That's why I ended up manipulated"

Chapter 4

Dealing with depression has ravaged many poor souls through all walks of life. I first started feeling down in1977 and my Mum and Dad used to think I was putting it on so that I was kept off school, and truthfully my reasons were usually 50/50, obviously I didn't enjoy school as I was bullied and I think that's when my depression crept in.

All through my last years of school I was certain it was a waste of my time because in my head I was going to turn pro then win a world title and buy a big house so my kids and dogs could guard all my fucking flash Mayweather motors. I mean when you look back at life you could say it hasn't turned out like that, only by a wee tad though might I add!

I think one of the biggest factors why I've suffered from depression is that I've always suffered from low self-esteem really very badly for years. When I split up with Bella's Mum Nik that was hard for me to get through. There's never been anyone that's even come close to replace Nik certainly on my part because she was the one. Then my insecurities tell me who the fuck would look at this big ugly boat race. I'm just a big bald lump, a big growler. Sometimes my thinking's are not too harsh on myself but I can be laid there at 3am and everything that is going through my mind is pulling me down. The doctors have told me I should be taking medication but I try not to unless my thinking gets too bad. Sometimes I can pull myself around with self-medication with a couple of glasses of wine, that helps me to sleep.

I know I shouldn't use wine as self-medication because it was something that caused problems in mine and Nik's relationship. The wine was beginning to make me more paranoid.

I'm what you'd call a "bag man" and I'd travel around the world with a plastic bag, that wouldn't bother me but that would embarrass Bella and her Mum Nik. The other thing in mine and Nik's relationship that changed was that I was old fashioned and I knew that if she needed money then I had go get up off my arse and have a fight! Maybe these days it wouldn't be possible because I'm 48 and I need a hip replacement. When I think of that it makes me feel old and I know my body is just about ready for the scrap heap.

I know I have nothing and just about everything I've ever done has been for Nik, Bella and Lauren (step daughter). I never ever tried to be Lauren's Dad only her mate, did I get it right? I'm going to say yes because I'm a bloke but sometimes girls need a Dad more than they need a mate but that girls turned into one beautiful young lady. I'm hoping somewhere along the line she says I had something to do with that.

Since my boxing came to a sudden halt about three years ago I've been able to hear my black dog barking and it could be anything that sets it off. My black dog has started getting louder because I'm putting weight on and that's because I'm not training myself, I'm only training Mikey and Ben. Them two boys who I train don't know how much they give me a purpose to get up and do my shit. At times whilst training them two we were out there in Spain for almost 18 months, backwards and forwards, that was a beautiful life and I'd have done that for fuck all never mind actually get paid for it. I sometimes don't know what I'd do if I didn't have them lads, Mikey and Ben, to get up for in the morning and I want to take them two cunts right to the top, I love the pair of them, deeply. God them two keep me functioning on a day to day basis.

I don't like watching all these real-life CCTV programmes that show you violent crimes being committed because I've lived through shit like that and viewing something like that would do my head in. My doctor has told me I suffer from post-traumatic stress and he told me going to counselling for that would greatly benefit me and I was booked in to go, that was until I bottled it. Yes, I bloody needed it at the time but I had a thing about not having that on my records. I know I sound like I'm mocking people with illness' but I promise you I think it's great everyone is becoming more aware of men's mental health.

There's a very famous scene in one of Ray Winstone's films. The film was a gangster type film called Sexy Beast and it featured Ben Kingsley playing Don Logan as a complete psychopath. Those of you that have seen it will know but I can so relate to that scene in it where he's looking in the mirror but having imaginary conversations with himself and getting more and more wound up saying such things like "he said what? Did he do that?! I'll sort that out for you mate it's no trouble!!!!! There's been so many fucking times when Nik has gone to bed and I'm up in the bathroom in just my pants having a fully blown chat with the mirror, calling everyone cunts and shit like that. Well I was only revving myself up for the next geezer who was going to ask a favour and usually it ended up with Nik shouting "OI SILLY BOLLOCKS SHAT UP AND BRING US A DRINK IN". Very rarely did I end up getting my coat on and off to see somebody but that was all madness to the highest degree. (Dom laughs)

Not long after the Audley Harrison fight I got a call from my very close friend B, after the usual chit chat he said "Dom I can't really hang about with you at the moment" well I thought he was just taking the piss but as the seconds passed by, it became clear that he wasn't. There I had one of my closest ever friends telling me that I was scaring him. Now this bloke was a big lump as well and apart from my old Dad, this geezer was one of the only men who I'd ever looked up to so it bloody hurt it wasn't just the shock, I fucking loved him. I felt like when I was in the nursery and somebody had just said that he didn't want to play with me anymore. I'll be honest you, I went home and cried my eyes out for three days. That was the first time I think that I started looking at myself. That bloke is an extremely close friend today and I'm glad we still see a lot of each other. He had asked me if I'd been fighting again and of course I had and blamed it on the others, but he told me that shouldn't be happening every fucking week! He had had enough I suppose and I can't blame him for wanting to distance himself from who I was at that time.

It takes a man to know when he's wrong but it takes an even bigger man to fucking change. Yes, I was getting a bad rep in and around London/Essex by people that I didn't give a fuck about, but I didn't realise I was getting the same bad rep with the people I'd die for. I'd become someone I despised I'd become the bully, I'd become just like Middlesbrough's Lee Duffy. The majority of my friends couldn't stand me. Some of my mates were too scared to tell me that they didn't want me in their clubs with my white trainers or training vest on. I'd just become used to doing what the hell I liked doing and I'm so ashamed it went that way.

I don't know how I managed to wake up but thank god I did. I now see how badly behaved I'd become.

Please friends and God, please forgive me.

"It's not what you are, it's what you don't become that hurts"

Chapter 5

The unlicensed scene I suppose was a case of beggars can't be choosers. Yes, I wanted to step inside the British ropes again but there was never any real chance of mixing with the British pro elite so I took it on the chin and got on with the level below professional level. It was a double whammy with the British Board because not only did I get called in for the head butt on Audley, but I cheated by using performance enhancing drugs. I promised my little girl Bella I wouldn't lie whilst writing this book so there you have it in black and white print. I put on a lot of weight and even if I'd have had my arm raised at the end of that bout it wouldn't have meant anything to me, I would never have deserved it. Of course, it flagged up anyway when I did a piss test and I received a ban.

To be honest at the time I was too arrogant to stand in front of the board and receive my sentence but I think I was banned for one or even maybe two years, but I didn't give a fuck. I was never planning on fighting under the BBBofC again, but if I had my time again I would have served my ban then I would have made a comeback.

Being truthful, it's took me over two years to put it right and get my licence back just so I could go in the corner with my two boys Ben and Mikey.

It makes me so fucking mad with myself that I played silly bollocks with the BBBofC because I was still in my prime years, but at the time I was too impatient, wanting to play the tough guy and being a brat. As I said earlier, I did the unlicensed boxing and luckily for me it suited my style of boxing.

The set up was a small ring and it was CRASH- BANG- WALLOP with small gloves. The referee would wish you luck and basically it was the last man standing. It was like being a kid again on the estates, whoever punched the hardest was the winner and the other went in crying to Mum and that suited me to a tee.

As I say, I was pretty much well suited to that style and I fought and beat the best from all over Britain. One evening I took on some full contact world karate champion, well 34 seconds into our contest he was sat there with his dummy hanging out of his mouth like a baby with a well smacked arse. He was taught a big lesson, we don't kick in a boxing ring mate, but if you want a go with Dominic Negus you'll get your face well and truly punched in. That's what a lot of them contests used to be, very much get in, do the business, get out and get your money.

Without bragging I was head and shoulders over most of them in that game and it showed when I only lost to the best of the best in Barwise, Williams and Bacon. My Dad was really ill when I lost to Barwise, in fact he died two days after so I couldn't give a fuck about the fight, but, I sold a load of tickets so I had to turn up and take my medicine like a man. I was well beaten on points. One of the saddest things I ever said was when my old man asked me about the fight, "How did you get on Dom Boy?" "I lost Dad, on points, but don't you worry about me just get yourself better Dad", sadly he never pulled through and that left me a broken man.

It's funny because there's a geezer in Essex who was going around saying Barwise only beat Negus because I trained him for it, not a mention of my old fella dying in the build-up though! Then when I went in and smashed him in the return fight he didn't mention that he trained Barwise for that either! When I took that first fight versus Barwise Freddie Roach could have trained me it wouldn't have fucking mattered, my head was up my arse. Then in the return I wanted my revenge and I wanted blood against Karl. I know it wasn't his fault, but he was the man who I had to tell my old dad had beaten me, I needed vengeance and thankfully I got it in the matter of just one round. The thing with that unlicensed circuit is that you meet people who aren't going to get the limelight. No disrespect but people like Carl Froch's brother Lee who's not really good enough to become a pro, now he'll never be Carl Froch that's why he's on the unlicensed circuit, but he's got the balls to get in front of over 1500 and have a ding-dong, that takes bottle.

My biggest problem was I was more than good enough to become a pro, but I done something very wrong and I had to pay the price. Yes, I wasted my chance in the pro game but let me tell you, there was better money on the unlicensed scene than in the pro game, believe me! I was bloody fighting monthly and I had a deal with the promoters, I'd always been a huge ticket seller see! What you do get more in the unlicensed boxing than you do in the pro ranks is geezers giving it the "big un" and you may only live like five miles away from each other. I had a fella who lived quite close to me and if he reads this he'll catch on right away it's him. Now as I say he was down the local gym at one point where my trainer Gary was at and he was telling every cunt what he was about to do to me, so my trainer Gary rang me up and enlightened me on his antics. Immediately I've got on the dog and bone to Alan Mortlock the promoter and begged him to make the fight! Within 30 minutes I had Billy big bollocks 'Uncle on the phone asking me what my problem was? Now I was right annoyed and didn't have a problem with anyone, but when some little nit wit is getting free publicity out of me it's not fair is it? I told him to tell his young nephew that unless he wanted to be serious about fighting me then to turn his silly games in, I didn't hear anymore from the bloke's nephew.

Another young lad who I used to work with years ago, all of a sudden started gaining a lot of weight and had started making a lot of noise about wanting to start a fight with poor old me. So, one afternoon I rang him up and told him I was thinking of making a comeback and did he fancy a few rounds of sparring? Of course, he said yes and I kidded on I hadn't heard his latest tales calling me out… HEH-HEH-HEH! Well good! "I'm on my way" was my response and I put the phone down. When I turned up at the gym above the pub I gave that geezer such a fucking hiding. I swear on my little girl's life, I only used 60% power otherwise he'd have been put to kip. I made a point of taking a few sparring snaps after sparring as well for social media so he looked very silly indeed. After our sparring he came up to me and said, "Dom can I please have a word?" I said, "Of course mate what's the matter?" He said, "What it is, is that I have never ever said I ever wanted to fight you!" I said, "That's funny mate because I've never even mentioned that to anyone!" That was a big lesson for him to keep his mouth closed!

Saying that, I'm 48 years old now and I haven't boxed for a few years. I think I'll always be able to throw a tasty right hand though when somebody's picking on someone.

I know today it's the 21st century and we live in a world of social media but even when I was boxing and there was no social media I would guarantee I'd sell the place out if you give me one month because they like me. In fact, even if I'm talking crap and people don't like me, people will always pay to watch because people love violence don't they?!

I was always very lucky when I boxed and people would pay to watch me fight up and down the country. When I was young and following boxing, I have stated many times, I looked up to Roy "Pretty Boy" Shaw and Lenny "The Guvnor" McLean.

When I started boxing it felt like I was born to fight and when I trained, I trained. Even though I lost a couple I was like a fucking soldier. Even if you beat me I never gave anyone an easy night's work. The only person who ever beat me truly was me, because I was such a fucking idiot or I'd allow things to get into my head beforehand. I give myself a hard time about that even now.

As I mentioned in an earlier chapter, I felt that I should have left Lenny to further my career, because me and Len were doing the same thing day in and day out for fifteen years! If Boy Jones Junior or Mikey Sakyi leave me tomorrow it won't be out of fucking boredom of training with Dominic Negus let me tell you. I've always been aware that those lads are only going to learn so much from one person so that's why I have them two fuckers all over the country sparring the best of British boxing. The one thing I feel very fortunate for now with my two lads is I've got them a few fantastic sponsorship deals. Maybe if I'd have had that financial back then I wouldn't have been doing what I was doing!

One of my favourite sayings in life is "I played the best game I could with the cards I was dealt". Yes, when I look back at the fighters of yesteryear I fucking kick myself. I'm forever looking at cunts and thinking, fucking hell I fucking paggered you in sparring or I was better than you, how the fuck did you win that title etc... I look at lads commentating on telly and think these cunts own several houses and I've got fuck all. I nearly went to prison and that was the difference.

"People sleep peacefully in their beds at night only because rough men stand ready to do violence on their behalf"

Chapter 6

As much as I could put in this book how much of a nice guy I am, there's no getting away that I've seen and been involved in monstrous levels of violence. I've had it done to me and I've done it to other people. Yes, I can say it was the bullying I went through as a fat kid with glasses, because it must have had some effect, but then again, my lad Ben Jones can fight in the boxing ring and is one spiteful fucker yet outside of the ring you couldn't meet a nicer boy who's anti-violence, so where does that come from?

My Mum and Dad were parents of the year they really were. They both were the best but when I got bullied at school I had to deal with things on my own as most of the time my Mum and Dad weren't even aware of the hidings I was getting because I hid them. Unless the marks were too bad to hide, then I would say I fell over in the park or something. This is where I can relate to them serial killers who have inner anger or inner turmoil, where shit starts to happen and they go off and do crazy things. You see all these docs trying to find out why Ted Bundy, for example, went off on a killing rampage and they put it down to when he was 7 and he had his dinner money nicked etc... Many times when I was at my worst in life and I'd deck someone, that only came about because I was thinking about something from my past. Sometimes if I was going to a job and I wasn't sure of what kind of environment or reception I would get, I would then set the tempo on purpose and go in and whack someone before a ball had been kicked so they knew I meant business. Half the time it could have been avoided if I'd sat down and thought about it.

As I've said earlier in this book I've had demons to face all the way through my life so it's always made me over eager to please people and make people like me.

I don't know what I expected, when I'd knocked somebody out, did I think for one minute that they were to stand up and think, fuck me he's a good man that Negus, I like him. If I wanted that then in fact I should have been at the mercy of a church begging Jesus to forgive me for my sins or asking some nutty religious cult if I could hang around with them so I had acceptance.

I used to have battles with my ego and pride. Sometimes when I needed my ego boosted I would go down my local boozer with all my fake mates. The tone of the evening was "NEGUS NEGUS you wanna drink"? Many of them used to stand me up in the pub and be like "see this man, he's fucking made of good stuff", when in reality those same people hated me and just used me. The very same people, when my back was turned, were saying "I can't fucking stand that big prick, fucking wanker! I hope he fucks off soon". I was told so many times what was being said about me by so called friends that I didn't trust anyone. I know I was a pain in people's arses, I do accept that but I was still feeling like just a little boy looking for love and acceptance but looking for it in all the wrong places. I just wanted to be wanted like a big puppy dog. I wanted people or somebody to put their arms around me and say, "come on Dom It's gonna be alright" and I never really had that, even to this day. In all of my years of participating in violence I was looking to be part of something, I know that might be hard to hear if you've been on the end of a clump but it's the reason I did it.

Of course, I'm very very sorry for any pain or suffering I ever caused anyone. My biggest weakness was in fact my strength because I could rip into someone and think, cor fuck me I didn't half catch him there, and people used to say they'd never seen anything like it when I ironed seven people out at one time apart from in films.

Now what I was doing could possibly have gotten me a life sentence so was that a good thing or a bad thing? Depends on the situation and who for! The geezer who was paying me or the geezer with five teeth missing?!

The boxing training only made me better at what I was about on the doors and when I started the debt collecting, In the end I became a sort of "paid tool" if you want. I was a bit like one of them excavators that you would hire for the weekend from a tool firm. Many people were like "ah we'll go rent Dom out for the weekend" and that happened! In the end I had such a reputation as one of the most dangerous men in London but in reality I was a complete fucking idiot. My reputation proceeded me and then it would be that I'd been suggested by a friend of a friend, so I'd be earning a few quid there too.

At the time the people I was associating myself with were all people 'in the know' and there was always something going on, a bit of skulduggery here and there. Sometimes it wasn't violence, I'd be asked to go watch someone pop to the bank as someone was taking money from A to B and I never asked questions, the less I knew the better for me really. This was how I provided for my family and work was never hard to find, in fact it followed me, and I was bloody good at it. On many occasions it wasn't even hard work it was more money for nothing, just to stand there and look handsome. One thing that would make me paranoid about looking like a wally was if I was getting paid enough. In the beginning, yes I had to accept £50 a job and get my arse smacked but it's like everything in life, if you're good at what you do you make it to the top of your game and towards the end of that career I wasn't getting out of bed for less than a couple of grand.

The violence back then was different and I'm only talking about maybe twenty years ago. These days in that game all you hear about is fella's getting acid chucked in their faces which doesn't even bare thinking about! In my day you got a right hander or if you wanted to be cute you got one up the middle (a punch in the guts so no marks were left). Listen, I was never a massive tool merchant but yes, when the game got tough there were certain things you had to do. Especially when you heard little firms where on the lookout for you and when they found you they weren't going to ask you for a game of hide& seek! That was another drawback about being 6ft 2, bald and handsome, as you can imagine it wouldn't have taken very long to find me would it. There was no point in me going to a knife fight with just my right hand &left hook because there would have been a little girl growing up without her daddy.

If you're thinking "Cor that Negus has been a right violent bastard". Well let me tell you that I've had everything done to me and it fucking hurts. It was part of the job description I'm afraid but it's no fun being stabbed I can tell you from first-hand experience, I definitely wouldn't have it on my bucket list that's for sure.

When my little girl Annabella came along in 2004 that was definitely the end for me and crime. Yes, even now when times are hard and I'm struggling to get the rent it does go through my head to slip back into my old ways, but it's only a passing thought. It's usually enough to ask myself would Bella rather see me this weekend in my house, or twice a month in Pentonville jail and that usually snaps me out of it. What am I going to do, take on a contract to get someone and the money's gone in a month? No thanks,

I'd rather keep digging the holes (training the boys) and see my little girl.

I often say to Bella I don't think I'll make old bones so let's enjoy the life that we've got. Bella's made me such a better person in life. Over the years I've met people I probably would have given a right-hander to but then they've killed the mood by saying "How's Bella?" and I'm like 'fuck off', I find it impossible to be annoyed now they've said that.

Nik said to me not that long ago she said, "You're a good man who has done very bad things" and she's right.

These days in pubs and clubs the violence is so freely given out now, people aren't bothered anymore and they'll cut you as soon as look at you. They're not bothered about going to prison and there's kids out there today 16-17 years old and they'll come and shoot you. I grew up looking up to your Lenny McLean's and Roy Shaw's who had straighteners and if they had a row with someone they had it on the cobbles, pure fisticuffs. That is a thing of the past now like the Dinosaurs.

It hasn't always been a walk in the park leaving that life behind. Even when I've tried to go straight and been honest it's been like pissing in the wind. One time I'll never forget was when I went for a job interview and the man who was interviewing me asked if I would beat him up if he told me off at work? The potential employer didn't give me the job because he was scared I was going to turn into a Neanderthal and I was gonna pull his eyes out. I do get the hump like normal people but don't presume I'm gonna kill you if we fall out! I've never hit anyone just for the sake of hitting someone and I never will. If things have broken out into violence there's always been a reason to everything I've gone and done. If there's anybody out there who has had a right-hander off me or has heard of someone who has then please question the reason. If I've put it on someone then it's never been without provocation.

A lot of the debt collection work I carried out was all above board and legal. What would happen was that a company would give me all their debts and they'd give me a percentage of however much I was able to claw back. Nobody likes to pay a debt collector do they? Not until you rag them a little bit and let them know you mean business but a lot of what I took on was above board which may surprise some people. At the end of the day they're the bad guys who are trying to rip the debt off, they're the naughty ones. Many a time they've said they've got no money which I've said, "That's fair enough, now let us work something out where everyone is happy" and I was more of a negotiator at times. Many times, I would let the customer decide which way they wanted to go about things first. If they wanted to be arseholes then they'd come to the right place. Sometimes people even put their hands on me first and I was just defending myself other times I've sat down with people and we've thrashed a deal out, then they normally say they never expected me to be reasonable because in their heads I'm just a figure of evil, when they say things like that it always makes me laugh! What do people think Dominic Negus does? Sit in the house and eat babies?

A friend of mines wife absolutely fucking hated me and she made it known, in the end my mate asked his Mrs just why did she hate Dominic Negus so much? Her reply was a very funny one, she said "My friend's husband was hounded by Dominic because he owed him money". To cut a long story short I'd chased down a fella who owed thousands and was blatantly taking the piss! But in her mind that was a good enough reason to hate me and hiss every time she saw me. At the end of the day you can't be going around blatantly ripping people off of their hard-earned cash can you, it's just life. If you're going to dislike me in life at least dislike me for the right reasons.

"Everybody says, a mistake is the first step of success but the real fact is, correction of mistakes is the first step of success"

Chapter 7

I got myself in a real big spot of bother in 2003. When I say big I'm talking as big as it comes i.e. 15 years in Wandsworth, two visits a month shit and as many letters as you can write whilst your hands not in pain from wanking. Around that time, I had a very bad six months in life, I got nicked for something, lost my Dad as well as being served up by them three angels in the gym sent to me from above. They say in life they'll be a point where three angels come at once, well this was my time and it took something like that for me to learn.

Before I jumped off the bus of violence and doing naughty things I was a mess. Mentally it was a very lonely life. These days I've been single for a good few years and I know it's down to not trusting people because of the life I was linked with. I realised who my true friends were only when I came out of that life. The friends who were around me when I got nicked, Dad dying and me getting bashed are still the circle of friends I have around me now. There's never been many new people that have come into my life, yes there's people I've had to associate myself with, like around the boxing world but I've never allowed them to get that close.

Going back to the potential trial though, that was looming over my head for a good six months and if that was going to go to court it would have been at the Old Bailey court one where all the most infamous of trials get played out. My solicitor told me that if I'd have been picked out of the I.D parade the old bill were going to remand me but I wasn't and thank god it all fell apart and I was allowed to live my life as a free man. That was really my saving grace and put me on the path to changing everything and even thinking differently.

It was after that trial collapsed that I was attacked by the three people in the gym. Now me and them three geezers are the only ones who really know what happened and it wasn't what was going around the grapevine in the criminal fraternity but sometimes you've got to let sleeping dogs lie. That's done and dusted and I'm not opening up no can of worms. All I will say on the matter is that I deserved what I got but not for what it was about and that's all I can say on the matter. What I will say for the record is, that incident with the axes, well that made me realise my life at the top of crime was over, this was my wake-up call. At that point I'd just started seeing through people who I was working within the crime world. My so-called friends weren't what I thought they were and I'm lucky to fucking still be alive. One friend who I'd like to give a mention to is B. That geezer saved my life just because he was there. I'll be eternally grateful to him. My friend Henry and his dad H also were there for me day in, day out during the trial before it got chucked out.

At that time, I couldn't really handle things considering I was supposed to be this "hard man". It came to a point where I'd had enough and things got on top of me and I even tried topping myself, I couldn't even do that properly though (laughs). At that time my nut was well and truly gone and it must have been about 3am when I was having fucking horrendous thoughts that were going through my head like the rush hour of London. I decided in a moment of madness that I would be better off dead, I cut myself and it was fucking horrible. I was a complete mess and thank god my mate Matt found me in his flat. I suppose the reason I'm still here now was the Stanley knife was blunt. The blood was pissing out of me though. Matt kept me at his house for a couple of days and told Nik what had happened. It all got sorted out of course because I'm still here but me and Nik have never spoken about that incident since. It's only because of the grace of god and my incompetence that I'm still here. I would never do anything like that ever again, so I don't need to talk about it. Don't get me wrong when I've been in dark moments and something clicks, people call it the black dog I think these mad thoughts, but I'd never deal with it on my own, I have my friends.

That's when a hell of a lot of people backed away from Dominic Negus because I was a runaway train and everything in my life was shit, everything I touched seemed to turn to shite.

Most days I was taking drugs and drinking heavily trying to forget that I was looking at a potential life sentence. One night in a nightclub just before the trial got dropped, I can clearly remember it, everyone was dancing about having a good time and for that second you'd have thought that I didn't have a care in the world. My mate came rushing over saying "god Dom we're having a fucking great time" and I was like "yeah we fucking are", because I'd pushed it so far to the back of my fucking mind it didn't exist. Then in the morning I woke up and that sickening feeling was back and it was crash, bang and back to reality.

I think the maddest thing ever was the I.D parade and just before I walked in I said to my new-ish girlfriend Nik that I had something to tell her, of course I hadn't told her about this case but before I could blurt it out she said, "And I've got something to tell you, I'm pregnant". Can you imagine that just being told you're going to be a Dad for the first time but thinking I'll miss the first ten years of the kid's life in some stinking prison. During the weeks after that my god did I pray to god, somebody up there was looking out for me. Now Nik's family are Jewish and they were going to the synagogue to pray. Nik's mum Lorraine used to tell me I was a good man and I'd only brought good things to her family since she met me, she prayed daily for me bless her. When I first got with Nik even her brothers Jason and Bradley pulled me to one side. They both told me they'd heard all sorts of Boston Strangler tales about me but they're nothing like what I am really about because I was a good fella.

Before the trial fell to piece's I promised myself that if I ever got out of this living hell, because I was convinced I was never going to get out of it, I wouldn't get caught even so much as jay walking. Even though I was innocent of what it was alleged that I'd done I'd seen people get stitched up before and innocent men have gone to prison. So, when it did thankfully fall through (and rightfully so) it was like God saying, there you go Dom old boy, you've got a clean slate now son! I know I was really well known to the police from my past, most of it silliness and shit I fully got myself into but this thing which was lumbering over my head for the best part of six months I was 100% innocent of and thankfully that came out in the wash.

The only good thing that came out of all the things I'd been involved with where people had got seriously hurt was that I was chosen, which sounds odd but it was a confidence boost back then. In certain situations people brought their best to the table then the other people would bring me to the table. I was basically the best man money could buy in a lot of people's eyes.

Your average man in the street never had anything to worry about from Dominic Negus, it was only fellow criminals or people in my world. I never took a fucking liberty with any straight man in my life. Of course, when I was in that world then the only stories going around about Dominic Negus were bad stories and I'll tell you why! Who wants to hear about how much of a fair geezer Dominic Negus is if you've hired him for a job? Nobody that's who. It was only the worst kind of stories people put about if they'd hired me or put me on some job to chase up. It's pure logic really. I've done a lot of bloody nice things in this life, helping people for charities etc... But nobody wants to hear about that shit where a character like Dominic Negus is concerned. The only people who really knew me were my handful of true friends that's who. I would purposely be seen trying to do good things so people would see it because everybody thought I was bad to the core. That's the time when I was so lost from the real me.

After I got chopped up by my angels at the gym and the court case collapsed I flew out to Tenerife with just me,

Nik, who was expecting Bella at the time and a friend of mine Lauren. I got rid of my phone and didn't wanna speak to anyone for a good while. Then the people from my old world all started asking about me, none of them could see me going straight like I was. People were saying all kinds of shit about me like "Dom must have taken too many blows to his head from the boxing", or "I heard he's found Jesus" even that I had run away to become a Monk! I couldn't give a fuck though, they could say what the fuck they liked, I'd seen the light and was walking on the right path which is what mattered the most. When I got back from Tenerife I went to see my friend Joe Egan at his book launch at Canary Wharf, Mike Tyson was there and was making a fuss of me asking if I was the legendary Dominic Negus from the unlicensed scene which was nice. Me, Mike and Joe had a bit of banter and had some pictures taken. Joe Egan's a very close friend of mine anyway and it was nice to have ten minutes with Mike Tyson and even nicer that he even knew who I was. On the way back from it I popped into one of my old drinking establishments. At the time I hadn't been in the place for a good eight months. I walked to the bar and all the old faces were there who I hadn't seen for ages. "NEGUS NEGUS" was the shouts from a few, like Neanderthals who had just discovered fire! A few came even closer to me saying "ere what the fuck's happened to you then"? I just calmly asked "what do you mean?" They told me "well we've heard you've changed and you've gone born again Christian!" I told them nothing of the sort had happened but what did it matter anyway? Then I said to a few of them there that when they had problems I was there for them, in fact I went to Spain for one of the fella's who was there. I said,

"Where were all you when I was having my bit of trouble?" There was an uncomfortable silence and I had my drink and I walked out.

There's times when I've had to rectify myself but I don't have to explain myself to anybody, especially those who thought they owned me like a robot or just a work tool and took the piss out of me and used me. I paid the price by having some bloody awful times and lonely nights and yes I paid my dues but now I was free.

This is what breaks my heart, the situation me and Nik are in at the moment. We're both on a break but we went through a fucking lot together at the beginning. Yes, a lot of it was put on by me like getting nicked on an aeroplane when it was ready to take off, that's just one example. She was my rock when I lost my Dad, then she was there for me when I got chopped up. Lots of people were saying "get rid of him" because she was a straight girl she didn't want that life.

After I was chopped up, that was the time I was suffering terribly from paranoia (I suppose three blokes coming for you with an axe, bat and gun would do that to you) because I was convinced they were coming back to finish the job after the pigs ear they'd made of it, it just made sense to come and get me off the streets.

My mate B and Nik were great and told me whatever way we chose we were going to fight this. I've cried and prayed with them two. At the time when my nut was going and I thought I was going down I asked Nik to move out to Tenerife but we'd have fizzled out. She was a straight girl and it was unfair for me to ask her to do that. Back in them days I was just too mad for her, but she stuck by me regardless and she's just the best mother in the world to my little girl Annabella. I couldn't have blamed Nik if she told me to fucking do one, one million percent. When I met Nik I knew I'd met a lovely girl who was all I'd ever wanted. I do hope we can work through it.

"When you're happy you enjoy the music and when you're sad you understand the lyrics"

Chapter 8

As a kid growing up I had a few girlfriends but I was never what you would call a hit with the ladies. In my late teens I met a lovely girl in Benidorm from Newton Aycliffe which is up North, called Debbie. She was lovely and I don't know what she seen in me I think she just seen me as her bit of rough. I actually moved up there and lived with her for a short while then she came and moved down to Essex with me but it never worked, we just fizzled out. I also got with a really nice lady named Lynsey and we still speak today and are good friends. I did get ladies attracted to me when I used to work on the doors but that life was never for me, the other fella's who I was working with got on with that but I'd always been a one-woman man. I was never really the player type. What I never liked about certain girls was the ones who only liked me because of the notoriety because some girls just love the bad boy don't they? Well I never ever considered myself as bad, I just considered myself unstable. I just couldn't stand people taking liberties and it made me get the hump.

There were times I would be in a club and having a lovely time when a load of loud, uncouth blokes have come in and caused mayhem and I've had to put a few of them away then the place has gone silently dead, then people are looking at me as if "what happened there" like it was all my fault! Well certain girls in Essex like shit like that happening! In all the years I've been with Nik she's never seen me throw a punch and if I had done, that wouldn't have impressed her anyway because that wasn't her thing.

Well I've met girls that have loved crap like that. I could never stand being psychoanalysed by females who don't even know me and they've told me that they could imagine me being in a bar and that if somebody chatted my girlfriend up that I'd be kicking them in the head. My reply to that was "God you don't even know me girl"! I never ever fought in front of Nik because it ain't right. Don't get me wrong there's been situations where it's been close and I've had to tell Nik to go sit in the car while I handled something.

I had an incident a few years ago. I was in a restaurant, and Nik doesn't even know this to this day unless she reads this, but something happened. Basically, a couple of people were being rude and I told her to go sit in the car whilst I went and paid the bill. When she was in the car I knocked two blokes spark out in the restaurant, got in the car and drove off. She doesn't even know about it because I didn't want her seeing that but it couldn't be avoided. I just could not handle those two blokes being so fucking rude on a Sunday afternoon whilst the football was on, those two fella's were behaving like animals and the table next to us never said anything. At first, I said "Oi lads drop it out, my Mrs and Daughter are sitting here" because we had Bella with us as well. The two fella's shouted back "ooh your Dominic Negus aint ya"? I told them I was and they needed to do their homework! To cut a long story short both fella's continued being pigs so I whacked the pair of them quick and left them both asleep on the floor. The next day I got a phone call and it was from the restaurant telling me I'd broken the fella's jaws and broken some chairs so basically they were after some money off me. I understood the establishments point and I went down and give them £150 out of my own pocket but it was well worth it.

Only last year a friend of mine asked me to back him up with a couple of fella's who had been messing him about and trying to take the piss out of him. As me and my mate walked in the two geezers who'd been giving him the run around were stood in front of us and believe it or not one of the men looked up towards me and shouted "cor you've put some weight on haven't ya?" and straight away it was "BANG" and he was holding his face shouting "WHAT THE FUCK"! I just told him if you've got nothing nice to say then keep your fucking mouth shut, we haven't come here to be sociable. The two fella's stopped taking the piss out of my friend from that day onwards and it was all sorted.

I have a really good friend named Bobby and he actually taught me how to box. He told me when I split up with Nik that 75% of men won't be going near my women because they're not fucking stupid. Don't get me wrong if Nik meets a nice fella then what can I say? She deserves a bit of happiness we both do. 15% ain't silly but they'll have a little sniff around like little sharks, then realise it's a bit too much that one because I can't just fuck it and chuck it! Kids are involved etc... The other 10% are fucking dogs and they don't give a fuck! They'd sleep with anybody and they would be willing to take the risk.

All I've ever wanted is to be happy and be with my family and it's really saddens me how it is at the moment. Nik wasn't my first love but she's been the love of my life and she's loyal. That girl stuck by me when other women would have run for the fucking hills, they wouldn't have come near me in the first place would they. Me and Nik got together in 2002 but I'd say we drifted apart around 2015 and we've been on a break ever since. She's the only person I love and I've not been with anyone else since we broke up. I know she doesn't believe that but that's the truth. I mean how could I get fixed up when I don't go out anymore and I have issues with trust. I don't trust anybody because there always seems to be a hidden agenda. If it was just me and Bella together for the rest of my life that would do me and I'd crack on.

There's still a few things I've got on my bucket list like visiting Australia though.

The hardship me and Nik have is we're both alike. We both mistrust and she's had a hard time with blokes in the past. Nik's been through the mill a little bit and when she got with me I had to pay the price and be patient.

When you go into a battle you need to pick a good army around you. You need a good general and sergeant. Well the people around Nik could be better. If you need advice you need a good source but Nik doesn't have that, not from someone who's been seeing a married man anyway etc… Nik's got friends that are so quick to judge and have an opinion but these are the same people that have split up other people's marriages. That's what I can't accept and I wish she'd change her circles if we've ever got a chance of getting back together.

If we were in Parliament and you've got wrongun No.1 and wrongun No.2 you wouldn't ask them for advice would you? I don't get people.

This isn't how I wanted it to be with me and Nik. I didn't want to be a single parent or a part-time Dad. Things have gotten in the way between us and of course I'm unstable and I get paranoid by things that don't even matter but I didn't want this. I know at times I didn't listen to her, can things change who knows? She's the only girl for me the only woman I love and at the same time Nik needs her happiness. If Nik feels the same way about me that I feel about her then it doesn't matter about anybody else does it, because they say that love always finds a way. Only time will tell. It isn't only Nik I miss, I was really close with Nik's mum Lorraine and her step dad John. John is the nicest bloke you could ever wish to meet. He's a typical ex docker and he knew all the chaps from Canning Town back in the day. John has done a great job bringing up Nik and her two brothers Jason and Bradley.

Nik never had to worry about other women ever when we were together, I loved her too much. I know there are times that she thought there was but hand on the bible there never was.

I always remember one day I was sat there with my guvnor at Top Man security Iain McCallister at a boxing show in Wales doing the security for the boxing. When all of a sudden I see these two ring card girls walking by, when that very second my phone starts vibrating in my pocket. I answer the phone and its Nik and she's telling me she can she me on Sky Sports eyeing up the ring card girls. I said what you on about? Honest to god I wasn't but Nik was telling me she could see me eyeing up a couple of slags. Sometimes when it was kicking off in the crowd and it was on the telly I would be scared to go into the crowd if there was birds about. That's how bad it got and I was only doing my job. That all comes down to Nik being insecure, exactly like me. My boss Iain thought it was hilarious.

I was very good at that job but it always meant I had to be away for the weekend doing the weigh-ins on the previous day keeping the fighters apart. Then the next day would be the fight then I'd be going straight back on the Sunday. I've been all around the country doing the big fights and Nik used to say, "For all I know you could be all around the country shagging birds". Well yes, I could have done, but I didn't! Nothing I ever said was good enough because it's what she believed.

What I will shout about in this book is how much that Nik is one fucking terrific Mother to our Daughter Annabella. Oh my god she's awesome. Them two are really close anyway and she makes me feel safe, work that one out?

Nik made me a lucky man because she gave me a little girl and that was the only thing I wanted in my life. Bella changed me so much. Yeah, today I'm still a little bit wonky and we all go a little bit mad as Anthony Perkins in Psycho said, but Bella gives me stability. She stops me from doing stupid things anymore. Of course, I still make mistakes, like the other year when I hadn't seen someone in ages and he'd robbed me so I gave him a little nut. As soon as I walked off, within two minutes I thought I shouldn't have done that, but in the world I come from yes you do because that's what people from that life understand. It's a universal language that everybody understands a fucking punch in the mouth, I don't care who you are. I've seen people coming up to me giving it "the big un" then a little slap changes everything. I've been to Spain, Italy and all-around Europe and seen many fighting men giving it large. Well I'm not into giving it "the big un". I'm into knocking people out though! Once you put it on a big mouth then nine times out of ten they'll shit themselves. In Italy and Spain they have the biggest shouters in the world, well I've never been into shouting. If you're shouting at me in the first place then you're being aggressive and I can't have that. If you cross that line with me you're going to get a dig and I don't care who you are.

I'm prepared to die for my family. A few years ago Nik rang me and said, "Dom somebody's trying to break into the house"! So, me and my mate Matt flew straight around the house to check it out but they must have gone. Another time Nik told me there was two geezers outside our house when we were living together so I went out and I saw two men up to no good. "WHAT'S GOING ON"? I shouted, both tried to look innocent but I told them that if they burgled any houses on this block then they were fucked! Both seemed game and were giving it a lot of back chat. One of them told me they were plumbers but I said, "Don't be a cunt, where's your van"? I knew they weren't. I said, "Do yourself a favour and fuck off" and off they went. Saying that Nik can look after herself and she never gave a fuck about me when I got the hump. She scares the fuck out of me when she gets going. Many times, I've been that anxious I used to shit myself going home, she was never scared to tell me what's what. I do hope me and her one day can have a future together but only god knows doesn't he.

I'd like to say sorry to Nik for the way things are at the moment. I'll always be friends with Nik but I think if we go our separate ways I couldn't go out with her and her new fella. I'd be too jealous and I'd be looking at him thinking I bet you're piping my woman later.

"Dom had a toe in both camps. He's a face and a proper person who can fight".

Steve Bunce

Chapter 9

Before my daughter Annabella was born in September 2004 my whole life was lacking stability. Me and Nik to be honest were quite lucky with Bella considering how mental me and Nik both are. As soon as this little thing come along I knew I had to change my life and what I was doing on a daily basis. The day Nik told me she was pregnant was a very worrying time for me. I think the words we both used were "I'm pregnant" and the other was "Well I've got an I.D parade". It was an extremely worrying time to think I might possibly miss the first ten years of her life.

Before Bella I could walk into a place and I know I was avoided by certain people. After Bella was born I could tell that those same people were glad to see me because everything about me had changed. My whole persona, my whole attitude to life went from one extreme to the other for the better and do you know what, she's such a good kid and I feel so lucky that I have her.

One of the hardest things for me at the moment with being on a break from Nik is not seeing our daughter everyday like Nik does. These days when I get the hump with people I have Bella in the forefront of my mind. I also think this fella who's being an arsehole could have a child who depends on him just like I do so what right have I got to bash him up over something so silly anyway. If I had to go to prison now then it would have to be for a fucking good reason.

Bella takes after her mum in the fact that she's just so funny and she's just so switched on in life. She's such a lovely looking kid, I mean everyone's kids are good looking aren't they but I really was blessed from god to have her. As perfect as Bella is she does have a few traits of her old Dad unfortunately. Bella can get quite upset at times so she's very sensitive just like myself. Apparently, I've been told she has a bit of a temper although I haven't seen that side of her yet. In the fourteen years I've been Bella's Dad I think I've only ever had to tell her off once, as in really shouting at her. My method is that I'll try to amicably discuss something with her in a grown-up way if I'm not happy about something and that usually works. Bella's like my best mate and we talk about all sorts and sometimes I talk to her about stuff maybe I shouldn't put on such a young kid, although the reason I do it is Bella will really tell me how it is, like the full picture. I mean most of the time I'm just one big kid anyway, so she probably makes more sense out of life than me. I mean sometimes I'll ask Bella her advice on a situation and she'll say very innocently "Just don't talk to them anymore Dad and tell them you're not their friend and walk off". It's so funny how she puts things and listening to her she makes it really simple for me. I often take her advice on board and sometimes I think it's her who is the one looking after me in life.

Only quite recently I had a bit of a disagreement with somebody at a boxing show and it was only because Annabella was there that stopped me doing something I would have regretted and fucked the whole show up. I don't want my daughter seeing me get the hump anyway! A huge reason why I've stopped doing the things I did in the past is because I know that if I ever went to prison, I'd be one of the ones who wouldn't make it.

Most of the time now the police don't even need witnesses because nine times out of ten it's all on CCTV somewhere. If I ever did assault someone and even if they said that they didn't want to press charges it wouldn't matter, all the police have to do is go to the CPS (crown prosecution service) if they've got me on camera giving some geezer a stroke then bingo they've got all the evidence they need and I get a nice five stuck up my arse. I just wouldn't be prepared to behave like that anymore and that's the reason I say Bella saved my life and probably a lot of other peoples.

All I want in this life is to give that kid a bright future and I have a lot of people falling over themselves to give her work experience in their places or a step on the ladder.

Bella's a very fit girl, into her gymnastics, athletics and at track sessions on a weekly basis. I don't want her stuck on computers all day so I've tried to encourage her to be into sport like I used to be once upon a time. I say to her that I wouldn't want her being dependant on anybody when she gets older. As long as she's happy and she makes her own way in life then she's got to do what Bella's got to do. There's just so much out there for the young people of today that you should never allow people to tell you that you can't do something. I tell Bella she can do anything she wants in this life and me and her mum will be 100% right behind her. To be honest I wouldn't want her boxing though like a lot of these girls do these days but I have taken her on the pads. Bella has always been around the gym atmosphere from day one with me, so I think the sporty lifestyle comes natural to her. After my pro career when I went on the unlicensed scene she was always in the gym with me on a day to day basis but above all I just want her to do her best in life. I want Bella to have a better life than what I had, I want her to have a stable life and I never want her to be like me, look at me now, 48 years old and I'm still worrying as to where the next bit of money is coming from.

The boys I train at the minute, Ben & Mikey, I'm looking at the bigger picture with them, I'm not saying that I'm just in it for the money but I'm spending the time with them and I want to take them to fighting at a bigger level. At the minute, if I never had their best interests at heart, I could have got them the bigger fights and really slung them to the dogs but that's not me and that's not what I'm about.

I'm in debt at the moment and struggling but that's something else I never want Bella to experience. I just want every day she spends on this earth to be a happy one and I don't want her to shed a tear, I want her to be friends with everyone. To be honest I'm dreading her getting older and life getting harder and more complicated when boys come on the scene, I'm looking forward to that chapter of her life...not! But that is life and it's going to come.

If I could live on a desert island with just me, Nik& Bella then I'd fucking love that.

If my Mum was alive now, I wouldn't be here now I'd be over in Italy with her where she used to live and I know I sound like an old fart but I would have loved to have lived out there with Nik& Bella, it's a better way of life out there, it's not like Britain. In England it's a dog eat dog world, fighting for the scraps all the time but that's not what I want Bella to be part of. Bella is not a violent kid at all but I tell her "if anyone has upset you that much then obviously something is going to happen".

My old man taught me how to fight without physically having to fight people. Now my Dad was only 5ft 7 and he was a proper man, worked on the print for 37 years, he worked every day of his life then he moved to Clacton. Now my Dad split with my Mum when he was 74years old, my Mum was 20 years younger than him, but he still looked after her even after they split up.

My Dad boxed in the Army but he had a way of fighting without actually fighting, he just had a way with words that meant he could get around the physical fighting and that's how I want Bella to be. My Dad was old school, he had been in the war and he had medals. Many times, I would hear my friends say my Dad did this or my Dad used to give us a whack but my Dad never did that, he just loved us. All my Dad ever wanted was for me and my brother to be happy in life and that is all I want for my Bella. My Dad was so good like that he would have given us the shirt off his back. He just wanted his Sons to do things the right way. Many times, when people turn out in life like I did, getting into fights etc, people always question your upbringing, well listen I had a fucking lovely upbringing.

In them days we didn't have a lot but Christmas' were great and we always had family parties with all the neighbours round. With cheese and pineapple on sticks and all that shit, it was great! People don't do that these days, if people have a party now guests turn up with a bottle of wine and a gram of bugle but I can't stand things like that, so I always try to be like my Dad, old school. My Mum was great as well she worked every hour and both of them worked their bollocks off for us. Usually we only ever saw our Dad on weekends. He was never in a pair of jeans and trainers he always wore a shirt, trousers and shoes.

"I hurt a lot of people in my past, normally every other day someone copped a right hander"

Dominic Negus

Chapter 10

Have I got regrets? A million percent I have cor yeah. The biggest one at the moment that eats me up today is the situation I have with my woman Nik. I never in a month of Sundays wanted to be a part-time Dad. Without Nik I wouldn't have had Bella and without Bella I wouldn't have seen the light.

A huge regret of mine also is with the boxing. I know if I'd have been more focused I could have been a proper contender. If only I knew the things I know now. Back in my day I never did the track work. The closest I ever did to that was run from lamppost to lamppost. Now and again I'd jog round a football pitch. I just got up to so much stuff a young boxer should never get involved with and I'm sure you can use your imagination.

Then again life could be a lot worse for me, like doing a life sentence. When I say that it makes me think of a good friend and former rival Gary Delaney from West Ham. Gary used to be a doorman and one night he was having a bit of grief in Woodford, East London, to cut a long story short punches started flying, Gary's hit the geezer who has then gone over. Next thing is the fella's went to hospital unconscious but recovered, until the next day when he's collapsed and died. Now Gary was only doing what I did every night of the week and that could have been me all over. Gary Delaney got a life sentence and was told he'd serve a minimum of eleven years. Well so many times many of my friends have said they'd have thought I'd have gone to prison for doing something like that rather than Gary.

When I was on the door incidents were happening like that every other day for me. All the young up and comers were coming to me to try out and get a rep because at the time I was the local magnet for trouble. So many times, my friends would pull up and say, "Hiya Dom who've you done this week?" It was horrible when I think back at the life I lived.

These days slowly but surely I'm creeping out of the cesspit. As I told you all in the last chapter I don't even want to think of me doing a 12 stretch in Pentonville. That's why I think in the last 15 years I've had one tug by the police and that wasn't even for me. They were just making some enquiries about someone else who I knew very well. That wasn't even anything to do with me. When I was finished being interviewed by the officer I told him that if I don't see him for another 15 years it couldn't be long enough. In fact, it was the same officer who'd nicked me on the aeroplane and I complimented him on how well he did his job then, but this time I told him I'm not in that world anymore so he was pissing up the wrong tree.

One of the big reasons I wanted to do this book in the style that it's been done was to give out one big huge apology to people I've upset and hurt in the past. If I've inflicted any damage upon you I'm so sorry. This isn't some kind of joke when I say that. There's an awful lot of people out there that I did damage to. I'm not trying to sound the tough guy please believe me when I say that. It's from a true heart.

Back in the day I knocked so many people out more than I care to remember. When you read these kind of hard man books of Britain's hardest men/Danny Dyers deadliest dustbin man you always get some geezer on the front trying to look terrifying, then when you open it he talks about how he knocked out 20 men in the one club. Well I'm not trying to say I was a hard man. If you want the truth then I was a fucking idiot. The reason I did Danny Dyer's programme in the first place was I wanted to get my point across to show people were I went wrong in life, but the way they edited that it never even came across like that and made me look more of a pillock.

Now I'm doing this book because I'm looking for redemption badly. If some folks can pick this book up, I just hope to god they can try to understand just where I'm coming from. I did in my past what I did and that can't be changed but if one person can see my point then I've done what I've set out to do.

There's nothing clever about the way I went about my life because you only get one go at life and I fucking wasted my career big time and I know it. I know there's a lot of people out there who haven't got the time of day for me obviously because of what I've done to people or they've heard a story or so on from someone they know. It's like if you meet someone and they've already knocked your best mate out then straight away without you even realising you think "that fucking Negus is a fucking tosser". What you've got to remember in my defence is that I never went around just fucking hitting people for the fun of it, like some blokes. What I was, was very free giving when I had the hump. When I was in a club and I was having an altercation with one fella but he was stood among five of his mates, I wouldn't just whack the one geezer they'd all get it. I didn't stop because I just didn't know how to in them days.

Many times, I've had a row with someone and it's exploded and when I've walked off, within seconds I'd be like what the fuck have I done there? My release button was so quick back then that I never really stopped to think about it.

On many of the doors in and around London you couldn't afford to not do anything because that was the difference between life and death. I could never stop to think 'oh maybe he's about to pull a shooter out on me' because that could have been fatal for me. Quite often, when I was having a bad day then the other shit creeps in like the darker side of my mind and then I'm all paranoid.

These days I'm a big believer in Jesus more now than I ever was before. When I was younger I didn't really care. There's so many times in my life that I've looked back and I'm so surprised I made it to 30. Then even more amazed I got to 40 and now I'm almost 50. In life things can change from day to day, hour to hour, minute to minute so sometimes you've got to have a bit of faith in what Jesus has got planned in store for us. I'm living proof for anyone reading this that there is light at the end of the tunnel. Every single day I'm alive I say a prayer and ask god for help. Many times, in life you'll meet people who don't believe in Jesus but as soon as something happens to them its "PLEASE GOD PLEASE SAVE ME" and I think that's very sad. That's like having a false economy in your life and I don't want that.

"Dominic took his eye off the boxing because of some of the other activities he was getting involved with. Had he not done that, then without a doubt he would have been a proper contender"

Steve Bunce

Chapter 11

Today in 2019 I just want a bit of peace in my life. Thank god I'm not where I used to be but a happy ending feels very far away at the moment because I'm literally living week to week like a lot of people.

These days times are hard and financially I was better when I was "at it" although not in the peace of mind department. All them years I was into debt collecting or just into general skulduggery I never had to care about money like I do now and I never took anything seriously. These days I lay tossing and turning worrying about my daughter or that I've got the rent to pay. It's a lot harder now than it was back then and I was breaking the law every other day.

I want people to read this and find out about the real Dominic Negus rather than the Dominic Negus that was in my first book. I have changed but I tell you what, it ain't half bloody hard! Especially when I'm getting offered to do things by people from my past most weeks. Of course, I could go do a job now for 30 minutes and maybe pick up two grand but I'm not prepared to put my liberty on the line.

Sometimes being this new peaceful pacified Dominic Negus sucks because Bella needs new shoes and is 14 going on 26. I hate not getting her nice things especially when her mates have the latest gadgets. Many times as an adult I have to go without because I get her things as I don't want her to miss out. My daughter deserves everything and if I could give it to her I'd give her the fucking world. Bella walks in my house and she lights up the whole place and she's more than I could ever ask for. To be fair to Bella she's not one of them kids who wants, wants, wants either. At times I tell her I can't afford certain things and she understands. That girl is my whole future and before I leave this planet, I want to know she's sorted out in life then I'll die with a smile on my face. I wanna see Bella with a good job, nice boyfriend and all the things I never had. Yes, I had a good upbringing from loving parents but I was never mentally stable. I'm still not now.

One of the good things I would say about myself is my manners are impeccable and that comes from my awesome Mum and Dad. That's one must that I have instilled in Bella because nobody can say anything about you if you have manners, right is might! If you open the door for someone and they don't say thank you I used to go "OI I'M NOT A FUCKING DOORMEN HERE" whereas now I'd just let it go and think how rude they are.

I think people in life have got the wrong end of the stick with me but at the same time I know I've given them a bit to go on in the first place. Then what normally used to happen is that I'd go on the defensive and change my persona like a big bear entering the room and give out bad vibes. A lot of the way I was just one big defence mechanism because once you get past all the bullshit I'm not really what you think I am after all. Once I feel settled with a person then I'm a real people person and I love to talk.

I'd say my set of friends has been the same for years. Certainly, since my first book 'Out of The Shadows' there hasn't been any new people coming into my life and that's the way I like it. I've been lucky enough that I have my best friend Bryn. I have another fabulous friend named Henry Smith who's a self-made millionaire. My two lads who I train Ben Jones and Mikey Sakyi aren't my mates they're more like family and Matt who I live with, we are very close, so I do have some fantastic people by my side.

If I could I'd choose my future to be awfully boring. If I could live on a desert island with just Bella, or maybe Nik as well it would be my dream, saying that me and Nik would probably kill each other.

For the rest of my life I don't think I want to step foot inside a nightclub ever again, god drop me out! I can't stand pubs also because I was told a bit of self-help from my friends that I'm like one of them old school style gladiators who perform in the arena. Well them pubs are the arenas or anywhere there's booze and drugs. I think for the rest of my life I'll be the alpha male and if I'm in them places I can't help but let people know that's my arena.

On a Friday night I used to go out drinking with a pal of mine called Alan, well we'd sit there and look about and if you've ever seen Lethal Weapon where you've got Gary Busey and he says "do you fancy a shot at the title"? and one of them goes "I don't mind if I do" well that was me and Alan every Friday night looking for these young up and comers who fancied a shot at my rep. Me and him would just look at each other and smile and he would say to me "Dom can you hear that"? And I'd ask what, then he'd say "the calm before the storm" and that's how it used to be and more often than not some fella would end up getting ironed out. Now I know that sounds bad, but I never went intentionally to cause trouble but as I said earlier, I was always wanting to impress people and that's how it all started.

Back in the day there was always loads of girls sniffing around me because that's what them girls liked, when in reality all the really nice good ones I scared away. The really sensible ones like Nik weren't impressed with that crap. When I got with Nik I think the reason we ended up together was she never knew anything about me.

How I really met Nik was that I used to go in a coffee shop she worked in every morning. Like I said Nik knew bugger all about me but what first drew me to her was that she always had this big smile permanently on her face and I was just drawn to her like a pisshead to a curry. After a short while I just kept going in there even when I didn't want a bloody coffee just to see her and we ended up getting together. I look at Nik now and I'm more attracted to her now than I was back then. She's like a vintage wine and she's just gotten better as she's got older. I'm hoping it will sort itself out between me and her, whether it will or not god only knows but I don't want to be on my own forever.

Like I've said I want things to change for me and my family in the next year and I want to be secure. I don't ever want to go to prison because that scares the fuck out of me to be truthful. I know the police would be on me like a dog if I slipped up and belted someone and I don't want that.

Quite recently I've had to go back on the sites working but the boxing will never go too far away from me.

My two boys Ben and Mikey have got big things in the pipeline. Those two lads have worked so hard for me and they're still only very young with big futures in the sport. Ben Jones is gonna go as far as he lets himself go, Mikey is going as far as his head lets him go. Both are very talented boys and I've also got Lyle coming through and he's about to go pro this year. Another boy I've got also just coming back is Butch Goldhawk and he wants to start fighting again. Last year I was training six pro's but things happened and a few of them wouldn't put the work in that was required. It's all or nothing if you're a pro fighter under me and a couple of them crossed a line that I didn't like. When you train lads who are a little older they like to do their own thing which doesn't work when you're under me. Another thing that pisses me off is if a fighter gets a loss then he's so quick to get another trainer. When I'm backing my fighter's careers I make sure we rub shoulders in gyms with Joe Gallagher, Ricky Hatton, Alan Smith, Tony Sims and Jimmy Tibbs. Now they're all great trainers and what I do is look at them so I can learn new things. With the boxing game you never stop learning ever.

"The fight is won or lost far away from witness'- behind the lines, in the gym and out there on the road, long before I dance under those lights"

Chapter 12

In April 2008 I was put on a job to look after one of world boxings biggest names Bernard Hopkins. He'd come over to Britain to PR his light-heavyweight contest with Joe Calzaghe.

I picked Bernard up at Heathrow Airport and my role was to be his shadow for 48 hours. I didn't leave Bernard's side until he went to bed. Can I just say now what a really intelligent man he is. My mate John was doing the driving and I was there doing the close protection. Bernard was just one hell of an interesting guy to be around for the whole time I was with him. When it was time to drop him back off at the airport he even gave me a $100 tip. As he was about to board the plane he waved me in close and said something very nice to me he said, "I could never see you but you were always there", meaning I was good at my job. Well that was just me doing my job. These days you get these fucking minders and all they wanna do is be in the picture. I mean I know a few people who were doing that work and were supposed to be looking after the stars but got kicked off the tour because they were too busy having a good time, well that's not in the job description I'm afraid it was never in mine. I was only there to do the job to get the star from A to B then back to A again in one piece. I mean if anybody manages to take a swing at your star then the fight could have been off causing millions of pounds to go down the toilet. What I should have done was got Bernard to sign that $100 bill but I didn't think. He also said if I ever wanted a reference for my C.V then to get in touch with him which was very kind of him. It really was just superb to be around him. Back then he was one of the world's top pound for pound fighters. If I'm being honest with you, I didn't even watch his fight with Joe Calzaghe which was very poor of me. To be quite truthful I like my boxing but if I've been around it all week then the last thing I wanna do is go home and watch boxing on the weekend. It was purely a job. I do have to admit I never even kept that $100 bill I changed the money and went home and bought a nice Indian meal in a shop called Spice in Barking for me, Nik and Bella. If you're reading this cheers for the meal Bernie. As we were eating that meal we were talking about how good of a guy you were.

Another colourful boxing event I did was when Nathan Cleverly was due to fight Tony Bellew at short notice. That ended in me picking Tony up when he was shouting to Nathan "LET'S DO IT NOW YOU FUCKING RAT"! I had to pull Tony to one side and saying to him "Tone what you doing mate, this is my fucking job!" I know Tony very well we go back years so he was cool. Tony assured me he wasn't going to hit him but I just couldn't take the chance, particularly as Nathan Cleverly told him to step outside in the car park so I had to pick him up and walk him out.

Another fighter who was always a little devil was Manchester's Michael Gomez, there was always trouble keeping him and his opponents apart. One memory I have of him was trying to put it on Ricky Burns in Glasgow at one of Alex Morrison's shows up there in 2009. Alex Morrison was there and he was really fired up and that fella is still a force even now he's into his 70's. I think I had to say to him "calm down Mr Morrison" because I think he wanted to put one on Gomez as Alex and Ricky are very close.

Another fighter you always have your work cut out with is Dereck Chisora because he's been in press conferences where tables have gone flying. Chisora and David Haye's fiasco in Germany in 2012 would have never happened had the fight been in England. Anywhere in Britain that would have been stopped before it started because me and the boys would have been all over them. In Germany there wasn't any big units paid to look after what was going on and it was a pure shambles.

I've been around so many top fighters in boxing but I think my favourite of them all was Roberto Duran. He was just an animal and one total spiteful little cunt. I met up with him only a few years ago at one of them 'Evenings with' and he was telling stories about when his fights were over all he was doing is going out, smashing brasses (prostitutes) and getting pissed and to me that knocked a little bit of the shine off him.

Ray Mancini is another fighter I would be in awe to meet because he brought me and my Dad closer watching his fights. Me and my old man watched a few of his wars and he made the memories that I have happen so to me he was an amazing man. I owe him more purely because the best memories of my Dad were being sat on his knee about 1982/83 shouting at the telly. Ray Mancini was supposed to be the new face of boxing but what fucked him was Deuk-Koo Kim dying when he boxed him god bless the fella. Ray Mancini had a massive influence on me as a fighter but also as a man. That man there was a proper sportsman and glorious in victory but humble in defeat. Let's be honest none of us in that ring want to lose but if it happens at least be humble then when you're on your own have a cry or punch a wall. I always made sure people never seen that side of me because people don't like that.

Now I'm not really doing the big fights anymore there's a fella called Jason Ashley (Bod) with a beard and basically he's taking my place doing all the big fights. Eddie Hearn and Frank Warren aren't stupid so they only use the best lads for the big fights. Eddie uses a company called S A UK and a bloke called Simon runs it, that's Clifton Mitchell's firm the ex-fighter from Yorkshire way. I'm not just saying it but when I was doing that we had the best team going. Now things have changed, it's alright being a big lump but when the shit hits the fan and the punches are getting thrown you've got to be on your game and I had a magnificent group of boys working with me, I'm not dissing any other boys out there that do it but I know who I wanted working alongside me in the trenches.

I was always very particular who I worked with and I'm not going to name names but there was a couple of incidents when I was stuck with people who could talk a good story but as soon as something kicked off I've turned around and they ain't there. I had that so many times. One evening working I got my eye smashed so badly because I was helping out another security company whose fella had been knocked out on the floor. Actually, I was working for Sky then so I shouldn't have been in the thick of things like

I was. That night I ran into a crowd to break something up and in the end a big bunch of men all turned on me and I kopped a whack. Afterwards I asked the fella where he was and he'd gotten up at that point and was stood watching. He even had the cheek to say to me he didn't want to get involved so I told him he was in the wrong fucking job. The promoter at the time whose show it had been actually paid me an extra nights wage because he knew I didn't have to get involved which was very good of him. I just couldn't stand back and watch innocent fella's getting the shit kicked out of them because all they wanted to do was watch the boxing. I'd hope if one day I was getting a hiding somebody would help me.

Over the years I've been really close to my old guvnor from that work Iain McCallister and for me he runs the best company in Britain called Man security. These days I look at Facebook and I see other firms saying "another top job we did this weekend and I'm proud of my boys" well I just think who gives a fuck that's what you're there for! People there know that if you've done a good job that's all that matters!

My team when I was doing it were Bod and his brother Jamie, Bod's a great fella to work with. Also, there was big John, Alex, Cookie, Isaac, Kevin Webster, Liam, Craig, big Al and big Colin, who has impeccable manners by the way, you could trust that team with your life. Not all of them are big lumps but one thing about each of them is they won't leave ya stuck. I've learnt in this world that you don't always have to stand and fight but you've got to stand tall.

One night I was working at an event in Wales and it was a surfing event it was so funny. Now all the surfers were all big lumps like body builders and you could see this event was for 18-30year olds and every fucker was nicking everyone's beer and things like that. So, this time we get a call to go and sort a big load of trouble that had broken out. So, we got told orders on the radio that we had to move this rowdy lairy bunch of drunks who were causing havoc and nine of us went down to where they were at. With me was big Chris and Liam and a few others and we just went in there and tore them apart it was so funny. I used to tell my lads to stick together, don't let anyone see there's a break in our armour. As soon as people see there's a little weakness that's when you get people coming at you like "COME ON THEN YOU CUNT". I remember one man running up to me shouting "look at you full of steroids"! I said, "Steroids ha more like cakes!" One bloke was even shouting "you're that boxer Dominic Negus aren't ya" as if he as threatening me to go to the old bill, I told him "as much as you know me it'll take me two days to find out who you are!" To be honest he had no right threatening anyone with the old bill because he was one of the main instigators giving it large. It turns out he was the local dickhead and a bit of a bully himself so nobody took no notice of him.

I can work with lads who aren't the best fighters but what I could never do was work with lads who wouldn't stand as one with us as a team. Oh my god I would never work with them again and they'd probably get a kick up the arse as well because I'm old school. These days if you stand up to troublemakers you got called a Neanderthal.

Many years ago if someone got cheeky with a doorman what would usually happen to you? I'll tell you what you got a slap. When I was growing up going in places I got a couple of slaps for running my mouth off. Then when I got to 18-19 and I got a slap I punched them back and kept punching them back. The mad thing is in all the years I worked the doors or security I got more trouble going out on my own. As a doorman you can try to defuse the situation but when I used to go out on my own it used to come to me and then I used to run wild and it was terrible.

"A deadly man exists behind his smile"

Danny Dyer

Chapter 13

In 2005 I featured in one of a series of documentaries called 'Britain's Underworld' and that was quite hardcore in a way. Out of the whole series mine got the best reviews because it was true life and it showed things didn't always go to plan. On one of the scenes it showed me training for a fight and lose the fight because my Dad was ill. My coach completely ripped the piss out of me saying I was an embarrassment but I didn't give a fuck because my Dad died two days later. I'm not making excuses but when I was in that ring I couldn't have given a fuck what was going on and I wasn't there mentally. Being in that ring that day it was easy taking the punches because it was taking the pain away. The fucking heart-breaking thing is I went to see my Dad the next day and he was sat up beaming to see me asking "How did ya get on son?" I just brushed it off and said don't worry Dad I lost but it was just a bad day at the office. I didn't want my dad worrying about shit like that but he died the day after I told him that.

That documentary showed me at my Dad's funeral as well as at the point after I'd just been chopped up by them three angels with axes and balaclavas. It was a bit mad it was showing me in the hospital. To be honest half way through that programme I wanted to give it a swerve because it was causing too much hurt but of course I'd already agreed to it hadn't I.

Going back to me getting served up, that all stemmed from me getting a lot of publicity off a lot of things at the time. I was getting too big for my own boots. At that time, I realised the people I was going about with weren't perhaps what I thought they were. It was always me doing the physical side of things when them fuckers were stood about chit-chatting. If somebody had to get hurt it was me being pushed in to having to do it.

Then in 2008 you'll have seen me on 'Danny Dyers Deadliest Men' but that only happened because of my close association with my friend Vic Dark being on the first series. They asked me to talk about Vic and when I was speaking with the film producers they just came out with "do you mind if we do you?" and I just went along with it, none of it was really planned by me for it to happen. I told the producers that the only reason that I was allowing myself to be filmed is that I wanted to get the point across that I don't really wanna be like that anymore but of course the cameras were only interested in me throwing punches on the pads looking like a monster. Again, Danny wanted to focus on what really happened to me in that gym with them three men because even today nobody knows who done it or nobody's owned up to that one on paper. I mean who's gonna own up to that because it was a complete fuck up. Whoever ordered the hit sent three of his best boys to sort me out and it didn't really go as they'd planned. All I wanna say on them three geezers who came into my gym that day trying to iron me out with an axe, baseball bat and a gun is that they got the fucking shock of their lives. Now I'm not wanting to open up old bygones, as I've already said, but me on my own, I wasn't what they expected me to be. Now there's only me and them three other fella's know what really went on that day and that's all I'd like to say. Nobody's owned up to it and if they did what am I going to do, sit there as a grown man and think ok lads fair enough I'll take that?!

Of course I'm not. Also, one of the biggest reasons I never found out who it was is because nobody was going to own up to the way it went down. If anybody said it went to plan well it never fucking happened like that. Also, if someone was going around telling their Jackie Chan stories of how they fucked Dominic Negus they know they'd be at risk of a comeback so that's why them people never said anything. I don't want to use the word embarrassing but if you've sent three alleged really handy fella's then you'd have expected the job done, mission accomplished. My good friend Terry Marley (god rest his soul) said to me, "Dom in my eyes you nicked that on a split decision". Three geezers all tooled up and I walked out of there that was definitely not in the small print of the job.

What you have in this life and certainly in that kind of life is ego's and pride and at the weekend all over Britain they're the two biggest killers! How much shit do you see on the telly now of the same thing where one guy is saying "you disrespected me man" then he goes and puts it on someone over something silly! It's all bollocks that people have to end up getting killed for shit like that.

You know something only yesterday somebody sent me a WhatsApp of a street fight over in Thailand where some geezer kills the other fella with this big fuck off knife and some fuckers stood there filming it whilst the poor blokes dying. Well what the fuck was the other fella filming it thinking? What about the geezer's wife and kids? It would kill me that would seeing something like that. Oh my god life's so worthless nowadays!!!!

I have to be truthful, when I watched the Danny Dyer program back I was embarrassed with a couple of things. I'm not having a go at Danny, Danny was cool and a genuine bloke. He even said to me "Dom I'm an actor I'm not a hard man blah blah blah" and even he was embarrassed with the way they'd edited it. Me and him had a conversation for about an hour and a half and it was really good it was but his producer never showed any of it. Even the cameraman at the end said "fuck me, that's probably some of the best stuff I've ever recorded" but where did it end up? On the cutting room floor! Even Danny told me afterwards "I'm so sorry Dom but the editors only wanted all CRASH-BANG-WALLOP". I told Danny not to worry about it and it is what it is, it wasn't Dan's fault. The bit where Danny asked me to demonstrate what happens on a debt I thought was really muggy. We went along with it just having a laugh, but I never thought they'd use them bits like that considering what they'd already got from me. The bit where we walk in and tell Danny we wanted the money I think we gave him a couple of dead legs but in truth I did tell Danny I didn't like that bit. I said, "Dan look I feel like you're mugging me off mate, is that what you do to proper people you're lucky I don't give you a right-hander". Danny told me it was just a bit of banter but I didn't like that to be honest with you. The stupid part out of the whole thing is I never even got paid for that programme, although I got a little bit of expenses i.e. food etc... I only did it in the first place to try and get my point across which I never bloody did. At the end of it all I just felt so short changed that the bit I wanted in never come across. It doesn't really matter now does it?!

It has put me off doing things like that in the future. Listen, I'm 48 years old now and I know what I am, I'm a little bit rough around the edges but I'm alright and I'm a good man. I've got fucking good morals! The way I've been brought up is that's black, that's white and they ain't no in between.

"To see a man beaten not by a better opponent but by himself is a tragedy"

Chapter 14

Boxing to me was my drug, or maybe just fighting in general for me because I used to get such an adrenaline rush every time I ever had some kind of punch up or even when I was just training. Of course I've taken drugs in the past but alcohol was one of my things, particularly when me and Nik were together. I would love bottles of wine, to be honest I wouldn't drink anything else but these days I don't really drink, I've had enough.

These days I need to get things straight in my head now so I can progress in life. When I did drink I would feel all happy one day and then the next I would feel a load of shit. Now it's no good for me and it's no good for my family. I've seen so many of my friends who were divorced going out on a Friday then the next day when they had their kids they were too fucked to do anything so I don't wanna be like that. Many times these days I'll go pick Bella up and we'll just go to the pictures and we have a great time completely alcohol free. A lot of the time, my own depression was only brought on myself because I magnified it with the drink and drugs. These days I maybe go weeks on end without drinking and but when I do drink I still get depressed so that's why I just try to keep away from it in general.

By god when I've been really bad with the black dog of depression it's grabbed me by the bollocks and its dragged me down. I remember once when I was living in my old house with Nik and we'd just done the house up, I was having one of the biggest bouts of depression I've ever had. I just went to bed and cried like a fucking baby. I had to get up in the middle of the night just to go look at Bella to tell myself that there was something worth living for.

That's when it's dangerous and you hear of people drinking bottles of red wine sat with knives next to their wrists. Take my friend Ricky Hatton for one, he's ravaged with depression. Some people wouldn't know to look at him though as he's always laughing and smiling in public.

Now I know the alcohol only fuels my depression and I'd rather just go get some fresh air. I know if I ever did something to myself Bella would grow up hating me so that's why I could never and would never do that but I do get so down, as down as I can be without wanting to kill myself. Some days I just need Bella sat next to me.

Another kind of drug ruined my professional boxer career and I can only blame myself. Steroids was the drug I used for the Audley Harrison fight. Even after I received a year's ban, one of my friends begged me to go to the British Boxing board of appeal and go face the music and say sorry and get my hands smacked. I was only looking at a one-year ban, but of course me being the idiot I said "BOLLOCKS! They can go fuck themselves" and I went on the unlicensed. Don't get me wrong I was earning good money and being able to pay the rent but looking back, my stupidity cost me my career! Nothing else. It wasn't the drugs it was just me being a fucking idiot. In life sometimes, you've got to hold your hands up and admit it and say, do you know what it was me! That's one of my biggest regrets and if I could change it I would. I should have just boxed at 15 and a half stone against Audley and it probably would have been a bit easier because I couldn't move as well because I was carrying the weight I wasn't used to carrying in a boxing ring. I don't know if I could have beaten Audley but I think I'd have definitely given myself a better chance without the weight. In that fight, for someone who used to be able to do ten rounds on my head, I was fucked half way through the fourth. One of the big talking points happened in the fourth when he knocked me down. Audley threw a shot and knocked me down and I took a knee, Audley has then taken three steps away then walks back and clumps me. Well he punched me when I was on my knees which really should have put me out but he never so that's how hard Audley could punch anyway!

To go back to the drugs, yes I've smoked cannabis and had my fair share of E's back in the day. The last time I had an ecstasy was about 2002 in Thailand and it made me just go straight to bed. What a great night clubbing I had that night. When you're talking about the gear (cocaine) yes I used to do that on a weekend but it was nothing like you see people hammering it, I would have a dab here and there but it was more the booze with me.

After the Audley Harrison fight, I gained some notoriety for about 6 months and every club or pub I went into people were chucking shuffles of gear at me. I never got to be one of them people who bought grams of gear and sat in the house getting mullered, I only ever did that when I was out to get pissed and keep me out for two days. Crack and heroin, fuck even going there. Drink wise I used to be a Trojan I could drink many people under the table but that's because of who I am, what I mean is I'm an addict! I'm an addict at life and I've got such an addictive personality so a little was never enough. Ones too many and a thousand is not enough for me and that summed me right up. I didn't like drinking everyday but when I did I was a monster with it.

When I split up from Nik I lived at the gym and slept in the ring because I couldn't afford to pay two lots of rent. When the gym closed and the lads pissed off I would sit on my own and have a couple of bottles of wine. Even though I would do that I would be up and showered every morning because the gym opened up at 6am. Not many people know that about me but I would get my sleeping bag out and go to kip with my clothes around the gym, it was a bad time of my life. When I had Bella at the weekend I wouldn't bring her to the gym I would always take her out or go to a hotel. A lot of that time I was also over in Spain too on and off training fighters out there, it was great. Many of the lads could never tell I'd been drinking the night before because I could always handle it well but I was just living day to day I really was.

The first Christmas I had on my own without living with Bella is the closest I've come to doing something stupid. I'd spent Christmas day round Nik's house for Bella but before I was leaving, all I wanted was for Nik to say, "Why don't you stay?" That would have made my Christmas but she never. Today Nik even says "Dom you could have stayed" but I know she didn't want me to. Walking out of that house was one of the hardest things I've ever done. I wouldn't recommend that to anyone. On the way back to the gym I stopped off at an off licence and got a big bottle of Jack Daniels and got back to the gym to put Ray Donovan on the telly. I was massively into Ray Donovan at that time. I was sitting there watching Ray Donovan and all that big bottle of Jack Daniels took was two hits as well and it was empty. I sat there looking at the big rafters in the gym and honest to god I was thinking "I wonder if it would take my weight?" I've seen a lot of people going through the same thing like that, Jimmy McCrory the gypsy bare-knuckle fighter from up North was a big help for me at that time and I don't even know him that well. Sean Toomey the Muay Thai fighter from Portsmouth was always putting things up on Facebook to help me on a daily basis. Another top guy was my mate, an Italian guy, Pascal from Peterborough who helped me so much. Them guys, to this day, don't even know just how much they helped me. I think that the further you go up North the harder the man gets, but down here we're more skilled technically wise. Sometimes skill doesn't even come into it it's a man's heart and they definitely breed them rougher up North. Boxing wise my style was that if it comes on top, chin down and hands up. It took me a long time to learn how to box but one thing I could always do is that I could always fight! Maybe that's the biggest reason I'm still here I don't know.

There's a saying in life by Mark Twain and its "no man is a failure who has friends" and I think it's out of a film called 'It's a Wonderful Life' and I so believe that. That film is about some man who's about to top himself at Christmas and life is all getting on top of him so he goes to jump in the river and some good Samaritan comes along and saves him but what he doesn't realise is he takes him back to how life would be if he wasn't in it and how it would have an impact on everyone he knew and showing him that gives him a reason to live, well that was so me at that point because between the friends that I have I'm always gonna get by in life!

In my life at the minute I'm winning but I know in reality I should be sat in prison doing a long time in a 10 x 8 foot cell somewhere like Parkhurst. I'm not silly enough to think that god hasn't given me a little break along the way. I'm not sat here thinking "ooh fuck people I got away with it". Believe me I'm very grateful things have panned out and I still have my liberty and I can see my daughter grow up instead of writing to her or seeing her in some shithole twice a month wearing a striped shirt. These days I've started to lighten up a hell of a lot and having a dry sense of humour even at bad moments in life can really help you prioritise.

"Boxers, like prostitutes are in the business of ruining their bodies for the pleasure of strangers"

Chapter 15

Bullying nowadays is so much more intense. Now we're in the 21st century and it's all the media stuff, texting people or abusing kids on Instagram terrifying them daily. The abuse I suffered as a kid was quite physical, people shouting "OI YOU FOUR EYES GIZ YA MONEY!" I would hand it over or I got the shit kicked out of me again! I would walk about with my glasses on in a pair of shorts and my white legs out and I was a tubby little fucker and people used to shout, "OOH LOOK WHO IT IS, IT'S THE FUCKING MILKY BAR KID" and that name 'The Milky Bar Kid' stuck from there on. Thinking about it I used to wear a cowboy outfit too so the kids used to give me belters so actually it's no wonder I grew up as angry as I was sometimes.

I was a very lazy kid and I would much rather be in the house and if my mates came around I'd try and bring them in the house so I was safe near my Dad. My Brother was the one who would be wanting to be out all the time but I just wanted the quiet life staying indoors so nobody could get at me.

Where I lived in Woodford there was just an overall meanness from the other kids. There was just so many horrible cunts I copped it from where I grew up. My school Woodridge was one hard school but was I bullied like kids are today? I don't know! I hated school and I can't remember a day that I wanted to go.

Everybody gets bullied in different way though don't they? Psychically I'm alright but it's the mental side of it even today I wear the scars. Bullies are very clever people and they manipulated me, making me do things I didn't even know I was doing so I suffered yeah.

All that did was just make me the person I am today and I don't like bullies. I was bullied but I was never knocked out and YouTubed like some of the kids today, especially some of the girls. That would absolutely kill me to see my daughter getting hurt by a group of kids but you know what would kill me even more, seeing my daughter bullying another innocent kid where they are all videoing it and laughing like some of the things you see on social media today. I have actually sat Annabella down and told her if I ever catch her being involved in something like that they'd be hell to pay, unless there's a fucking good reason for it. You've heard these kids being bullied something rotten then the next thing the kid goes home and tops themselves at 12 years old. That would break my heart. I just want Annabella to be a nice girl. Which she is as far as I'm aware. She's awesome, with good manners and my friends love her.

If I drop dead tomorrow I know they've got her back. Annabella is my hero. Bella has got numbers in her phone of my mates Henry, Brynn, John Kershaw, Ben Jones, Mikey Sakyi and Micky Theo they would all help her at the drop of a hat. I've told Bella that if she's in trouble at all and she can't get hold of me or any of my friends then she is to call the police.

When I got a little bit about myself as I got older and I could look after myself I'd go out on the Thursday and come back in on the Sunday. Probably all the insecurities I have in life have all stemmed from being the little fat kid with glasses and when I got older I wanted respect. It wasn't really until I was about 19 though, after I'd lost weight and started working the doors in Essex that's when I would say I could handle myself properly.

I'm a leader and I've never been much of a follower. These days I just don't tolerate shit and if I'm unhappy with someone I won't even answer the phone to them. It's not all about the fighting no more it's about using my head. If I don't let them people near me then I can't do anything wrong in the eyes of the law.

"Dominic Negus is proper old school. I fucking love Dominic I think he's great"

Terry "Turbo" Stone (Actor)

Chapter 16

Tenerife is a real naughty little place and anybody who's ever been will know what I'm talking about. After the Audley Harrison fight that was the place I fled to for a bit of peace and quiet. My brother had a bar out there and I had a lot of people out there offering me work. Sometimes I was on the door and I would be fighting three times a night. I was like a pig in shit!

All the money I ever earned inside the boxing ring I used to call my "flash cash" because of course I earned a pound note doing what I was doing outside of the ring.

I had a good friend called Joe out there who didn't drink, smoke or take drugs so what I used to do was go about with him and I always felt rehabilitated and I'd go home fully relaxed. Then again whenever he went back to Britain and left me in his house I just got up to mayhem having parties galore. I'd like to apologise to Joe because whenever his back was turned I used to play up. I caused havoc in one of his bars and knocked a good few people out a few times so that was a really terrible thing to do.

When I was out there, as I've already stated, I was as happy as a pig in shit because every single night in those bars in Tenerife there was hell on. The place was like the old Wild West. It's all changed out there now but back then most bars were like the bar in Star Wars and most nights people were getting knocked out and dancing on tables.

When I was out there, there was an incident where someone had one of my friends over for some money. Well one afternoon I was in my Brothers bar when my Brother shouted to me "Ere Dom there's that geezer who had so n' so's money away". Straight away I ran over to him and grabbed him, I told him "I want my friends fucking money" and I told him he better stop taking the piss. I was quite fair with him and I gave him until the end of the week to pay up but he made no effort at all. So, the day after the date went by for him to pay I was in my Brothers bar again, I think I was actually on the karaoke giving it the "big un" when who walks past? Yep that's right the fella who had my mates money away, walking past looking like he didn't have a care in the world as proud as a fucking peacock. Well I couldn't believe his cheek and I actually had to double check it was him because he looked like he just didn't give a fuck. I waited until the break in the song then ran over and walloped him and left him out cold on the floor then went back singing for the next chorus. Well my Brother was stood there gobsmacked then he's pulled me aside and said "Dom this is a family bar, you can't do things like that in here" but I didn't care because of the damn front of this bloke taking the piss. It was a good few grand, I know it wasn't my money, but I was so annoyed that he'd had one of my friends over I just couldn't stomach it. It did get sorted out in the end after that and he paid the money that he owed.

These days in Tenerife it's very different and it's been thoroughly cleaned up and all the rough dives have gone now and been replaced with new trendy bars opening.

There was a few boxing camps out that way also with Naseem Hamed's family having a place out there then you've got the TKO Canning Town lot also over there. Nigel Benn also used to stay out there but I never ever saw Nigel.

I would be backwards and forwards between Britain and Tenerife for a while. If I was fighting on the unlicensed scene I would come back for that, have my fight then bugger off back to Tenerife. I had some great, awesome times out there but very mad with the things I was getting up to. Sometimes I would be walking down the road and I'd realise it was 7.30am and I'd think, shit I haven't been to bed for two days! Then I'd perk myself up and be off to Lineker's Bar then mostly end up back at people's house parties. All this was fuelled by a bit of help (if you know what I mean) I'm not proud to say that. When you're so up you can't stay there and of course what goes up must come down and I had some comedowns out there where I'd get myself all depressed. I mean you can't go on a two-day bender just on the strength of being a fit motherfucker do you know what I mean?! Even though I was in a different country, many times people would come up to me saying "Ooh you was that boxer weren't you"?

One day that I don't like to think about, I was in one of the bars in Tenerife and I was up by the pool table when some geezer came in eyeballing me for 20 minutes. In the end he sneaked up behind me after walking all over looking at me and I ended up putting him out with the pool cue. He was making me all edgy. I even asked one of my mates "is that bloke looking over wanting trouble or what?" My mates said, "You're right Dom he is".

When he woke up he killed me because the first thing he said to me was "I thought it was you Negus I only wanted your autograph!" I must have said to him a hundred times "I'm sorry" and "I was all paranoid" but the worst thing about it was that he had a red pool que mark right across his forehead. I just thought he was coming to put it on me. It was survival of the fittest over there.

Another time over there I had to go see someone debt collecting with a friend who'd had the piss taken out of him. Well anyway we walked in what was this fruit shop and asked the bloke "are you so and so?" Now my mate was worse than me back then and he commands respect, so when the bloke in the shop turned around to him and said, "Hold on mate I'm busy"! I just flopped him straight away just through my eagerness then jumped over the counter to do him more. My friend was screaming "FOR FUCKS SAKE NO DOM"! My mate didn't want to hit the man he was trying to do this one legitimately, but I couldn't stand him being so rude. The funny thing is the bloke didn't even turn around when he told us to hold on, he just thought it was some joe public.

I was earning a nice few quid over there, but I wasn't drinking every day, but when I was on a bender I went for it.

One of the best days of my life was out there when we'd been partying in Bobby's Bar and we walked out of there about 7am. I was with my good friends Danny and Paul and maybe a couple of others and the sun was shining, I didn't want that time to end. We'd laughed all night, but all walked into the light towards home. We all ended up going back to our apartments for two hours kip and then back out to Paddy's Bar and back on it again.

"The first time I met Dom he came in my gym as a skinny blonde curly haired youngster wearing glasses. He told me he wanted to learn to become a fighter, the rest is history. I've never changed my opinion of Dom since the first day I met him. We'll always be friends"

Dominic's former boxing coach Terry O'Neill

Chapter 17

I know I fucked my career up well and truly, but I was too busy being a cunt, but in my defence I was a good cunt because you don't want to be a shit cunt do you?! I was too involved in everything but the boxing and it so upsets me at 48 years of age to look back and know that I blew it.

Looking back, I sparred with everybody and there were some proper champions that I was just as good as if not better in the gym.

Boxing has been good to me friends wise though I'd like to say that. I know some lovely people because of boxing, like Andy Ayling (even though he's hard to get hold of on the phone), Boy Jones Junior (Ben), is like my son and of course Mikey Sakyi. I used to be really close to my old amateur coach Lenny Butcher but he's doing his own thing these days. Some people in life can't accept change and in boxing you've got to have change to keep learning. There's no point doing the same stuff week in, week out because you'll never get any better will you?!. Another couple of guys I've been close to are Peter Fares and Albie Turner. Both guys have helped so much with Ben Jones' sponsorship and they've even been coming into our camps with new ideas. Another top fella, he's gone now, god rest his soul, was Dean Powell. Me and him were very good friends and we would spend a lot of time together. Most weeks I would phone him for advice for the boys before a fight and he would help us. God that man is so, so missed. Frank and his son Francis Warren have also been very good to me so they both deserve a mention. In boxing sometimes you can't help but know everyone because it's such a tight community. People I definitely would call my friends are Jimmy and Mark Tibbs, both I like a great deal and they know so much about the sport. Tony and Peter Sims are also great boys. Alan Smith and Harry Andrews I hold in such high regard. Joe Egan another top fella. Mike Jackson and Ricky Hatton, Mike is Ricky's right-hand man and one of my closest friends in boxing. Dennis Hobson always gives me words of wisdom. I don't know how he knows but often when I'm down he rings me to perk me up and is always inviting me up North with him. I have to be careful naming these names because I'm likely to forget someone then somebody gets upset.

In boxing it isn't all hunky-dory because fuck I have met some dogs in boxing. There's a lot of people in boxing that try to make it look like they have done a better job in boxing then they have and I'm not talking about the fighters either! Boxers are boxers but there's other people away from inside the ring that tell a lot of lies. In boxing if you lie you get found out, that's the way it has always been.

A lot of things that go on in boxing have opened my eyes I've got to say. The one thing about me is I'm very loyal but if you fuck the loyalty thing with me then it's gone. When one of my boys is fighting all I'll wanna know is what date he's fighting, what weight he's got to be, how many rounds it is and when can we have the tickets. I'm quite simple to work with but there's so many others out there that want to have so many things in their favour its untrue.

I'd probably have to say my best memory in boxing was winning the Southern Area Title. When I beat Lincoln's Chris Woolas for a British Title Eliminator in September 1999. I was at my best ever then and done everything perfect. The thing I would like to make clear was that even though I fucked things up with the boxing I never ever missed a training session, I would be training every day. It was just that I was too busy doing other things in my head. So many times, I would be in the gym and I'd say to my trainer "I've got to be out of here at 7pm Len because I've got a job to do". That should never have been the case. I was more bothered about going to knock on someone's door at 8pm for a debt than what I was doing in the gym, that ain't right. That was my thinking and I wasn't focused enough. Listen I used to train like a motherfucker, but you've got to be focused which I never was, ever.

When I lost for the first time it was to Hackney's Bruce Scott in nine rounds and that broke my fucking heart, but what that did was make me realise I was a top top fighter. At the point I faced Bruce he'd won 19 fights and KO'd 17 so that fella could punch. Bruce never hurt me in the fight but what he did do was split my eye and the ref stopped it. Gutted wasn't the word but it's one of them things in boxing. I have a lot of respect for Bruce Scott because he was the one who changed my way of thinking towards boxing. Even though I lost I turned from a boy into a man that night. Bruce made me realise that I could compete at that level.

These days I do get the odd boxing fan coming up to me saying "Are you Dominic Negus?" straight away I'll say, "Is that good or bad?" and then just laugh. I still have that thing in my head that when people ask if it's me I think that it's for the negative reasons but really, I need to remember that there's better in me than bad and I'm a good bloke, I just did a few silly things! In my head I don't know if I've hurt someone they know or "you've knocked my dad out" is coming. I say to Bella sometimes, "it's not always the good people in life that have books written about them darling". Bella made me a better person. Bella made me see the light.

"If you are having a ruck with someone then you would want the likes of Dominic Negus around but then again if you were having a nice party with nice people then you'd want Dominic Negus hid under the stairs"

Dominic Negus

Chapter 18

Today I spend very much of my time guiding my two boys Ben Jones and Mikey Sakyi. Ben Jones just walked into my gym at 15 years of age off the street and he's never went away ever since. He's such a loyal kid and he's learnt in life the hard way. He actually didn't have any amateur contests only a handful of unlicensed fights. Ben was never made for the amateurs anyway like I wasn't. He's actually just became a Dad and he has to put the work in because it's not just for him anymore he's providing for a family. Ben has had so many fights cancelled this year, so he's had to go get a part-time job as well as continue his boxing career. I have so much time for Ben and talent wise he'll go as far as he wants to go.

His boxing name Boy Jones Junior was thought up by Frank Warren's right hand man Andy Ayling because there was already another Ben Jones in his weight from Crawley so that's how he got the name Boy Jones Junior which sounds like Roy Jones Junior doesn't it! In another four years Boy Jones Junior will be more well known in the boxing world. He really lives the life a boxer should, and I can't ask anymore of him training-wise. My two boys Ben and Mikey have given me another reason to live, as much as my Bella has because they're the reason I get up on a morning. I'd die for them boys and I'm always on the phone to people trying to get them a better angle moneywise or getting them some more quality sparring.

Everything I do in boxing is for them or my other boys Lyle and Butch who are also going to be two pro fighters very soon in 2019. I just wish I had the people around me like I am now when I was boxing or somebody with only good intentions.

If I ever got to the point where I thought I couldn't take my boys to the next level then I've told them all I'll introduce them to a better coach. I tell my boys if they've done as they're told, and they fuck up then they can blame me. If they do it their way then they've nobody to blame but themselves.

Ben Jones has only just left the Super Featherweight division and moved up to the lightweights, but you should see the size of him. He's 6ft and very rangy and he can really fight. To look at him you'd think he'd like to box at range, but he likes to go in and have a war toe to toe in the trenches. He loves to rock 'n' roll like one of them little Mexican fighters and loves a nice left hook to the body. The fight he lost to Suffolk's Craig Poxton was because he was lacking the man strength that Poxton had as he was almost 10 years older than Ben. I didn't really want that fight in the first place but after the fight we went back to the drawing board and put it down to a learning curve.

Mikey Sayki is another one who's a natural talent and he's the current Southern Area Welterweight Champion. He's probably better than Ben skill wise but we call it "nigger slick". I don't mean to sound racist but black men are far slicker than white men everybody knows that! Mikey doesn't have an ounce of fat on him and is incredibly gifted. My only worry for him is that he suffers tension and anxiety before a fight like we all do. At the moment he's working with someone called Nick Kemp from Leeds who's a life coach and he's so good. The sessions that I've sat in on with Mikey has opened my eyes to a couple of things because he's so good. There's big things to come from Mikey Sakyi in 2019 remember the name. I want him fighting for the British title in 2019. I don't like Ben and Mikey sparring each other anymore because it tends to get too out of hand.

I do take them boys all over Britain training wise. We go up to Hyde in Manchester for bits with Ricky Hatton or to Joe Gallagher's in Bolton. My lads have done dozens of rounds against top fighters like Paul Butler, Joe Cordina and Anthony Crolla etc… The one thing I don't do with my fighters is keep them in the same gym because they're not gonna learn anything that way. They need to learn the confidence that it takes to walk into someone else's gym and do the business, I've even took them as far as Spain to go sparring with champions out there. As long as my boys want me I'll be behind them a million percent.

We have a laugh together we have a cry together we're like one big family in my gym. When Mikey fought Siar Ozul for the BBBofC Southern Area nobody gave him a fucking chance, so at the end when he knocked him out in the 10th round I was so emotional and when I ran in that ring to pick him up I was crying tears of joy. Them moments will stay with me for the rest of my life and they will for all of us.

I've sat down with Ben Jones and Mikey Sakyi and I've told them I'd love to be them. I'd love to go back in time and have my moment again in boxing because they know I fucked it up so because of that I won't watch them fuck up the chances they've been given.

So many people over the years have told Ben and Mikey how lucky they are because of the things I do that other trainers wouldn't do for their fighters. The one thing I tell my fighters is whatever you're doing, don't give up! That could be 100 metre sprint, swimming or bag work. If you're gonna quit things like that then things are going to get a lot harder in the ring. One of my fighters did it to me out in Spain once, he was running around the track and when I asked him what the matter was he told me his legs were hurting. I told him that he couldn't do that in a fight, and didn't he think the other boys that were running around the tracks legs weren't hurting? Of course, it's fucking hurting it's meant to hurt, and I told him "you ain't got it mate!"

The one thing I can't stand is negativity and I don't like it around my fighters. As soon as anyone negative comes around my camp I'll stand up and say you've got to fuck off! Ben Jones told someone to fuck off away from him not long ago because someone was whinging he's got a four rounder whilst Ben's got a ten round title fight coming up and he was so right to do that.

I've seen mollycoddled fighters and fighters with a bit of talent but that haven't got the heart for the fight game. There's so many different attributes in boxing today and you need a bit of everything to succeed in the game.

When a fighter is making up excuses to me in the gym then I know I've got my hands full. Then again some fighters you need to mollycoddle because they can't cope with the outside part of being a boxer like selling tickets etc... He might be the best fighter in the world but just because he can't sell a ticket doesn't mean that he's still not worth taking a gamble on. It's up to me to know my fighter when he's a bit down struggling with his Mrs or when he needs a kick up the arse. One of my fighters Lyle didn't turn up the other month for training because his baby kept him up all night and it was actually Ben Jones that bollocked him not me. Ben said that's what babies do and it's not Dom's fault and he was dead right to do that. My lads are a team so it's no good one of them not turning up because it affects the whole mood in the gym. If there's any young fighters out there that are willing to give me what I demand in the gym then I'll take on any young fighter because that's my job.

In boxing the biggest problem we have is not being able to sell tickets. I've seen fighters who are not that good but when they fight they can sell 300 tickets and they are the ones the promoters look after because that boy has filled literally half the arena.

Mikey Sakyi and Ben Jones are a pair of cunts, but I love the pair of them and I'll stand by their side in battle for as long as they need me.

If you wanna follow both my boys on their journey you can do so via Twitter @Mikeysakyi and @Boyjonesjnr

Ben has his blue tick on Twitter and everything so that means he's proper famous.

"Our greatest glory is not in never falling, but in rising every time we fall".

Chapter 19

For many years a good friend of mine named Spencer Murphy ran a club called The Blue Mondays in Essex, I used to be the bane of his life just because I'd step foot in the place. Back then I was such a naggy cunt but the last time I seen him I could tell he was genuinely pleased to see me because I've changed so much since them days. My whole persona has changed, and I no longer walk around like a bear with a sore head waking up from three months of hibernation. I don't want to mug myself off here but the fact of the matter is I was so bad in them days. My daughter these days calls me a bear so I'm happy being a big old bear but a very different one from a few years ago.

My friend B used to say, "come here Dom let me look in your eyes today" and when he'd look he'd say they were full of fuck and he could tell I had the hump that day. I'm hoping these days people see me different to what I was. Sometimes I know I can come across a little unapproachable even though I don't mean to be.

When I was with Nik she would always say I talk to people like I was down at the gym and sometimes I know I needed to be pulled up on that.

In 2019 these days I walk outside and I can smell the grass and look up at the sky or I'll stand and enjoy listening to the rain. Back 20 years ago I would be oblivious to all of that because I was too busy looking to punch some cunts lights out. Back before Bella was born I'm sorry to say but I wasn't a nice person and I can hold my hands up. Today I know even some of my friends have said "Oh Dom you weren't that bad" but I know I was, I wasn't very approachable at all with anything in life. I didn't just have a chip on my shoulder I had a full bag of spuds. Before I changed I used to look at people in life with nice things and I wanted them immediately whereas now I know you've got to work hard for the nice things in life.

Now I'm no psychologist and I'm not making excuses for the way I was but looking back at the issues I had in life must have stemmed from the bullying I received as a boy. It was certainly never the way my Mum and Dad brought me up because that was only ever A1 from the day I was born. Yes, I was a sensitive kid, I always took everything to heart and I would get upset by a lot of things. In my eyes anything negative that happened during my childhood was from school. Looking back, I was the angry kid who stayed indoors when everybody was out playing football trying to be the new Kevin Keegan. I had so much inner-anger and I think that's why I was so angry as an adult and being that angry would lead me to taking anger out on the wrong people.

Sometimes I can lay in bed and when I think of some of the things I've done to people in the past it makes me cry. I have cried looking back but some thing's couldn't be helped, I mean with the debt collecting the only reason I was turning up at your door at 8am was because you've caused a problem, I didn't do that you did! That was work and that was purely work but the other things I have to hold my hands up to. I'll admit that yes I was bullied and then I became the bully myself and I hate myself for that. I flung my weight around and thought I was the bollocks in Essex and I'm lucky I never got killed.

There was a bloke up North from Middlesbrough called Lee Duffy and his life was the mirror image of the way mine was. He was bullied and then became the bully and ended up getting himself killed at 26 years of age. That's what was about to happen to me if I never walked into the light, I'm sure of it.

Being attacked with bats, axes and the rest I should have, at the very least, been badly injured but I was lucky enough to walk away with the few scars I have. The day I was served up by them three fellas well, they made their point but if I'm being deadly honest with you I think that was a message from above I promise you. Nik at the time was pregnant with Bella and so I changed my life dramatically or I'm sure I'd have meet the Grim Reaper well before now.

As I've already said when I walked away from that part of my life people didn't want me to change. People wanted me to still be that bad Dominic who you could say to "There's that cunt who's robbed me of five grand" so I'd go "I'LL HELP YOU OUT" then BANG!!! Back then that's just what I would do because I was a big people pleaser and I put them before my needs because I thought I was worthless.

A few years ago I was in one of my mates' houses and some fella come in and started bullying him. Now this geezer was a big old unit himself and he was giving it the "big un" something about a fire in his back garden. Now when the bully came around I was in the back kitchen so he couldn't see me but I could hear him scaring the life out my mate for no reason whatsoever so that's when I intervened and said, "What you doing you cunt?" Basically, I chased him out of the house but before he went he even stood there and kissed his bicep the prick. I didn't hit him but I told him to piss off and off he went in his car, then two minutes later the police turned up. The geezer was alright trying to bully my friend but when I've spoken up he's ran off and called the police the muggy cunt.

Sometimes I think I'll always have a little bit of that side about me even when I'm 88 years of age stinking of piss. I'm saying that with a big smile on my face as well. If it means that I'd no longer stand up to bullies and liberty takers then I'm not sure I'd wanna change, well maybe just a little bit (laughs).

I've got to be honest with you I don't think I'd ever wanna be without what makes me stand up for the underdogs in life. I don't think as old as I ever get I'll hide in the corner from anyone but I don't want to do the things I've done in my past.

At the start of this book you'll remember reading the story about how I heard those three men in the toilets slagging me off, well something similar happened exactly the same about 12 months before that incident. I was in the toilet and I heard some bloke saying, "oh that fucking horrible Negus is in here" and when I heard him I smashed his face into the window because he was slagging me off and he didn't even know me. He was a right flash cunt stood there slagging me off all in designer clothes but it's things like that I'd wanna change looking back. You can't go around beating the whole world up can you because somebody doesn't like you even if its unjustified. Although he was having a pop at my mate as well but still that was nothing to do with me was it. I left him on the floor and I told him to go do his homework on Dominic Negus ya flash cunt but I can't paper up the cracks. I had such a huge chip on my shoulder in them days.

There's things I done that didn't need to be done and I'm so sorry to the people I did wrong to. I was forever policing the area and I would take people's problems on that weren't even mine. Some men in Essex will walk in a bar and have a good scan around and see who's about, then they'll know if they can take a liberty. Usually if they see me on the door they'd think "oh we'll leave that bar for tonight" because I was more trouble than it was worth. Sometimes if I was in my mate Spencer's bar I didn't give a fuck and anything could happen that night. That's a bit muggy on my part I know. People knew I would be there most weekends if they ever wanted to find me or try to cause any trouble.

I've never been one for dressing up when I've gone out to bars, I've always been very happy in trainers and T-Shirts but when I was with Nik she was always into her fashion. My attitude was always that as long as Bella had things then I didn't care. When we were all out together I always felt I let the side down a little bit because I was Mr scruffy bollocks. Nik used to say to me "Dom I could make you look so much smarter in a suit and shirt" but that was never me.

These days I'm out in Essex and I grew up out here but I was born in Bethnal Green within the sound of The Bow Bells. That makes me as Cockney as they come doesn't it and I'm very proud of my true East End roots. Boxing and villainy has always come from the East End in anyone's era and I suppose it always will. I suppose looking back coming from East London we were very fortunate to grow up in Woodford, Essex rather than the East End slums because it's not the old East End anymore. The days of the true Cockney have well gone, there's so many different cultures out there now that there's seems to be no traditions left and all the old real ones came out to Essex and Kent.

Growing up in and around London, boxing comes to most kids at some point in their life because it's just the East End's way. I was always active with the boxing even when I wasn't in the gyms. Most kids in the East End have been in a boxing gym at some point in their lives, even if they didn't like it.

I really learnt to fight at the Leytonstone with my friend Bobby Wilcox who taught me how to box. It was just an open gym you pay and you play, that sort of thing, and that's where I also met my good friends Mark Wilson and Gary Bedford.

"Dominic Negus had the potential to be a lot better than he ended up being in the ring there's no doubt about that. Whoever Negus boxed, and he did face some good fighters like Audley Harrison and Bruce Scott, he caused them problems. Dominic Negus gave everybody trouble and it was a real shame that he took his eye off the prize"

Legendary boxing writer Colin Hart.

Chapter 20

My Dad, Cyril Walter Negus, was the straightest and nicest bloke you could ever have met. Me and my mates used to finish the nightclubs and often come back to our house at 3am and my old man would always come down the stairs with his aches and pains. Dad always seemed to have a bad leg but he'd shout, "IS THAT YOU DOM BOY?" and he'd come down and put the kettle on for me and my mates. All my friends loved my dad and even when we used to bunk off school he'd say, "Look come home at least that way I know where you all are". Most things in life my Dad done right then I come along and I'm a fucking scallywag. My brother Frederick was like my Dad as in a straight everyday bloke but I cut corners in life. Even though me and my Brother were so different Dad treat me and him just the same. In the end when my Dad moved to Clacton when he split up from my Mum he knew what I'd been up to the last few years. I think it dawned on him what I'd been getting up to because when I used to visit him he used to tell me a lot of the things he'd heard about me. I think the words were "COR FUCK ME DOM BOY YOU'VE BEEN UP TO ALL SORTS AINT YA"? People used to go up to Dad regular and say "oh your boy was at it last week in a nightclub" etc... I was very fortunate and my Dad and I had a chat before he died. Just before he died I went down his place in Clacton and it was the only time I ever spent down his place. That night I sat and talked to him and I knew the end was near. What I did find out about Dad though was a hell of a lot of things he did in his life and I said to him "Dad how come you brought me up to not do this or that but you did so and so?" Dad just smiled at me and said, "Fucking hell Dom boy I've had a fucking life!" I mean he spent so many years in the army at war so he must have seen so much gore. I know a few things happened to dad but he didn't like to talk about them but I could sense there were things behind his eyes. My Dad used to have terrible nightmares so it didn't take much working out.

I only ever wanted to be like my Dad but I just couldn't pull it off because I was so different. For instance, my Dad went to work 9-5 but I didn't want that I wanted to be a leader! I wanna go around Australia I wanna go around the world, I mean we're all gonna be dead soon and I wanna at least take some memories with me. My Dad, in general, was just easy going and we always had clothes on our back, shoes on our feet and food on the table. What more can a kid ask for growing up in the 70s, nothing. Me and my brother were showered with love but these days it's harder because there's so much shit in the world going on and most kids have got to keep up with the Jones'.

Dad's death broke my heart and it still does even to this day and fuck me my old man's been gone over 15 years. My Mum, Stella is another hard one to take. If I'm being honest with you I've got, or did have, a lot of resentment towards Mum and that's purely because she left my Dad. I just wish I could have half an hour on a bench with Mum in Heaven to talk to her because today it still kills me. Because I loved my Dad so much I couldn't see any reason for Mum to leave Dad but of course me and my

Brother didn't realise just how bad the situation was in the background. I was living in Newcastle then so it must have been around 1994 but I got a phone call from Frederick my brother asking me if I'd spoken to Dad lately? My response was "No why?" And he just hit me with "Mums left him!" I said, "Shut up you loon our dad's 75 years old, what do you mean left him?" I put the phone down immediately and rang Dad, he picked the phone up and said, "you've heard then?!" Well I couldn't believe it, people just don't split up after over 30 years of marriage and this was Mum and Dad! I said, "What the fucks going on dad?" Dad just told me it was down to Mum having a midlife crisis at 55 years old. Dad was 20 years older than her. Dad told me Mum was hanging around with a younger bloke etc... Well listening to my Dad tell me that, especially at my Dads age, was devastating. I mean that would be hard to take at 40 years old but at Dad's age it was magnified. What do you tell someone who's 75 years old when their wife's left them, "oh just crack on son", yeah right! Looking back maybe because Dad was 75 and Mum only being 55 they were two ships sailing past each other and Mum had a bit of life left in her I don't know. At that time in his life my Dad would usually be sat on the sofa, fag in his hand or he'd fall asleep with his teeth hanging out but that was my Dad. Usually if he was asleep he would still know if you went near that telly and he had the reflexes of a cobra. Dad would love all them programs like News Round. When dad was sat in front of the telly he was the boss and of course in them days we only had one telly in the whole house. I had this unbroken respect all the way through my life where I wouldn't even raise my voice to him, he was the boss. My Brother was different to me, even though he was different to me he was still a naggy cunt and he used to shout and scream with Mum and Dad. I'll never forget one Sunday afternoon my brother Frederick was playing up in the hallway and I walked past and barged into him on purpose. Well the next thing is Fred's done his nut and came and squared up to me screaming how he'll have me, next thing Dad's got in between us both and pushed me away because I was the one who instigated it then my Brother went to hit my Dad. Then Dad's given him a backhander and put him on his arse. That was all my fault really and I ran and locked myself in my room.

If I can be half as good as my Dad in life for Bella then I know I'm gonna be alright. Don't get me wrong my old man Cyril could look after himself but he had far more upstairs then I have in them situations. Dad was forever sitting me down and saying, "Dom why do you need to fight all the time because one of these days you're gonna come out second best". My answer was always the same "Yeah but I'll be the fucking closest second they'll ever have" and that used to really wind him up. Of course, I was young and full of myself and always thought I knew best but I didn't.

Dad worked every day of his life and gave me and my Brother everything we ever needed. The thing about Mum leaving my Dad really kills me and I never really got the chance to talk to her about it. I mean why did she leave my Dad? There was nobody better than Dad! My Mum did have another boyfriend called Chris and he was actually a hell of a nice fella, but he wasn't my Dad!

My Mum, at the end of her life, battled cancer as well as a triple heart by-pass and I was guilty of not realising just how bad Mum really was. At the end of her life she moved over to Italy to be with her family because Mum was Italian. Out in Italy they have a much better structure out there where they look after their families much better than here in England. I knew Mum would be looked after well by her family when she was out there but I always remember getting a phone call a couple of days after Christmas but just before New Year's Eve saying that I'd got to get over as a matter of urgency. Straight away I flew over to Italy, which cost me around £1500 even though I've known friends who've got a £90 return flight. Them airlines kicked me in the bollocks, I also knew I would be going to see Mum for the last time so the full trip was just awful it really was. All the time I was there my mind was racing and I was thinking what I was going to say to her for the last time. My brother Fred was already over there. He did better than me in that situation I have to admit. At that time if I'm honest I just wanted to be like an Emu and stick my head in the ground because I couldn't cope. At the time there was mention of cancer by the doctors but I didn't really understand Italian so it went over my head. Maybe I'm using that as an excuse I don't know. Mum had also been suffering with a bad back, I think her spine had gone as well so things weren't looking good. All Mums cousins were at the hospital and there was an interpreter so I was only picking bits up from the conversations I was hearing. It did turn out it was cancer of the spine, I did get to see Mum and to be honest things had picked up with her so I went home because I had a fight scheduled on the unlicensed scene. My plan was to go home get the fight out of the way then fly back and spend a couple of weeks with Mum. Even Nik was saying "look Dom you need to get yourself back over pronto" so that was planned until I spoke to my Brother Fred on the phone. What Fred told me regarding Mum's situation was very positive indeed so I held off going as quickly as I was going to. In fact, they even sent Mum home which I thought was great news but what I didn't know was that if you're terminally ill in Italy they send you home because what's the point in dying in a hospital bed and taking space up. Even when Mum had a triple heart by-pass she was sent home and all of her family had to donate blood. At around that time me and Nik moved house and my Brother was still over there. That day I was moving house I actually had my Mum on the phone and I told her to give me a couple of days and I'd be back over. A couple of days later I was at the gym doing a bit of training for my fight which was coming up and when I looked at my phone I'd had seven missed calls at 6am so I thought what the fucks all that about? All the calls were from an Italian number so I rang Fred immediately to ask what was going on. Fred didn't have any idea what was going on so I phoned one of my cousins up and they told me to get a flight ASAP to Napoli airport because Mum didn't have long. Straight away I've rushed home from the gym, Nik had already got me a bag packed because I called her on the way home and told her what was happening. In the airport going through customs I was waiting for the pull by the authorities and of course they didn't disappoint but not for the reason you would think. I'd taken one of Bella's pink Snow White bags and as I was going through I was asked "what you doing with that bag?" Straight away my gun of an attitude was loaded and I've just shouted "WHATS THE FUCKING MATTER? MY MUM'S DYING AND I'M GOING OVER TO ITALY TO SEE HER FOR THE LAST TIME". People were looking over like they do when there's a scene at an airport. As I walked past I said, "Do you wanna look in the Snow White bag" and the fella very subdued just said "It's ok off you go". I know I had an attitude that day going through customs but them men who pulled me didn't have any idea what I was going through! A little empathy could have been used by them fella's that day is all I can say.

As I was waiting for my flight I was having a couple of glasses of wine at the bar before boarding the plane, thinking that maybe Mum was pulling my leg and it wasn't as bad as it seemed, they were the hopes I had in my head anyway. I mean all Mum's love a bit of attention don't they? It turns out that this was no scheme and that this was real. I lost my Mum before I got to see her again. To this day my regret is that I should have given Mum more attention and if Mum was alive today I'd be over there living with her in Italy. I am gutted, absolutely fucking gutted I lost her in the way I did because my Mum would have so looked after me. If my Mum knew that I had spent 18 months sleeping on a gym floor my Mum would turn in her fucking grave knowing that! I feel so guilty for saying to my Brother Fred that maybe Mum was revving us up and I've got bills to pay beforehand. When I was in that situation my friends B and Henry Smith looked after me and told me not to worry about money. They just said to go out there and that we could talk about money when I got back. The way I found out Mum had died was horrible. I'd had a sleep on the plane and as soon as I got off the plane my cousin was stood there and the words "sorry" to me said everything. My Mum had died one hour before. Well I stood in that airport and I cried like a cunt! I got in the car and I saw my Brother there and I just cried, which I was rather embarrassed about. I was trying to keep it together in front of him. I phoned my mate B up and he said, "Is everything alright Dom?" I just said, "No mate she's gone", he said "pardon" I said, "Nah mate she died an hour ago". It was a bit hard that one.

I went to see her when she'd passed and my Brother walked in first, the full family were there as it was an open house. They do things differently over there as I've told you. As soon as I seen Mum I went do-lally and I was punching myself in the face going mad, screaming. I don't know what I was doing, what was it I was looking for sympathy? I was upset obviously but I had so much anger and I'd felt so cheated that I was just one hour late. Then I was feeling bad because I should have been there, that's the thing that kills me today. I should have been there! It doesn't matter what anyone has told me over the years like Nik and my mate Ian, I should have fucking been there. I flogged her off because she had her family there over in Italy. I just told myself that if Mum was that bad they'd have her in hospital by now but they never. Did I just tell myself that to make myself feel better? I mean she was only 72 when she went! I carry that guilt to this day.

Regarding Mum's send off, my Uncle told the funeral directors that nobody was to touch her only me, my Brother or my Uncle and they understood. He wanted it that way. I had to pick Mum up and put her in her coffin and that was the worst thing I've ever done in my whole life. I could have picked her up with one hand because there was nothing left of her because of her battle with cancer.

The night before Mum was buried I had a drink with my Brother around the coffin and I couldn't help but think Mum was gonna pop up shouting "WOOOOOOO". At times I was shitting myself because I've watched so many horror films. It just didn't sink in my Mum was dead. The next day they took her to the church and considering it was such a small town where she was living everybody came to send her off. The whole town walked behind her and the next day they had a big mass for her. Mum was put into a tomb and that's where she's resting to this day. When it's my turn to go that's where I wanna be buried. I wanna be put in the same plot as her because my Dad said, "you've always got to look after your Mum". That's why I feel bad because I feel that I've betrayed Dad in a way. When Mum was ill I wasn't there for her was I?

In the village where Mum lived in Miaori, people are born there, live there and die there, when I used to go over within one hour everybody used to know I was there because everybody knows everybody's business. That ain't a bad way to live and it's so peaceful over there, I wish I was out there now. In Italy they don't live like we live worrying about shite. The Italians don't have a care in the world. I don't think over there I'd have trouble sleeping thinking that someone was going to come for me or that the old bill were gonna nick me or even how I was going to pay the rent the next week.

"Between the radiant white of a clear conscience and the coal black of a conscience sullied by sin lie many shades of grey where most of us live our lives. Not perfect but not beyond redemption"

Chapter 21

Growing up in Essex in the late 70s all the local hard men were huge names. You had your Roy Shaw's and Lenny McLean's. These were names that you couldn't avoid growing up as a young impressionable kid. Them fella's were who I looked up to as a boy so with that in mind was I ever going to grow up any different? Sometimes when I was in nightclubs around Essex and people would be like "FUCK ME THAT'S ROY SHAW OVER THERE"!

I was honoured that Roy Shaw agreed to do my foreword for my first book 'Out of The Shadows'. People used to say "ooh there's that Lenny McLean he's a bully" but I never really knew Lenny that well at all but I've been quite pally with his son Jamie. When I'd gotten to the stage of my life were I'd made a bit of a name for myself I remember once Jamie McLean gave me a lift and before I got out the car Jamie said my Dad sends his best and that meant something to me at the time because that will have been when I was only around 26 and only concerned about making a name for myself, foolish now I know, that was when Lenny was ill with the cancer.

You wouldn't wish cancer on anyone whether people growing up in Essex loved or hated them men either way they were hugely respected as men and they could really have a tear up.

When I was in my 20s in and around Essex I was slowly but surely creeping up the ranks because I was fighting so regular and my name was being used all the time for bad things. Now looking back I know that wasn't a good thing. Physically, yes I was hard but mentally I was so weak and that was always my problem.

"Yes, a dark time passed over this land, but now there is something like light"

Chapter 22

I want my future to be different from my past. I don't want people to be edgy when they see me from now on. All that shit is in my past and today I'm a very different man.

These days when people come up to me and talk boxing or Danny Dyer or that they've read my first book it is very positive. A lot of feedback from 'Out of The Shadows' was super positive and I don't think I've read one negative comment regarding that book and it did alright sales wise. My old Mum even had a copy over in Italy and it was so funny. She'd always be showing people over there saying "that's my son" bless her.

Regarding my future I'm not wanting to rule out living happily ever after with Nik and Bella. Bella's always been in my life, look (Dom points to his right arm) I have Nik's fucking name tattooed on me and I don't regret it. I'll always be in Nik's life regardless of whether we're together or not because she's Bella's Mum.

One of the things I've only learnt recently is that people care about me, but they also care about my Daughter, so if I'm not the one for Nik then she's got to be careful about introducing someone else who is going to be around our Daughter because if anything ever happened to her, that's the only time I'd pull in every favour from people I'm owed. If anything happened to Bella and I couldn't do anything about it then I'd put it onto every cunt who's every owed me a favour that it had to be sorted. Nine times out of ten I wouldn't have to because Bella brings a lot of light into people's lives and she's a little bundle of joy. Even though she gets the hump sometimes when I don't agree with her but that's only because I'm trying to teach her what is right and what is wrong.

Only the other week I had a bit of grief and the first person I went to for advice was Nik at her work. It kills me because I just want to be her friend I wanna be with her. She tells me she loves me but that she doesn't want to be with me! Maybe it's my fault in the first place because it was me who moved out over three years ago. At the time I had a few things on that I had to handle and I didn't want her involved. I needed to do it on my own. Nik never ever got it and she said she didn't believe me but I knew what was going on, she didn't. I dealt with the scenario and maybe it wasn't such a problem in the first place but now it's done. The other issue I suppose was that Nik used to say I didn't get on with her daughter Lauren but I done so much for her in her life, now she's telling me I don't get on with her daughter after brining her up for over a decade. What I did have a problem with was Lauren treating her Mum like shit and the house like a hotel. When I was growing up I was always told by my parents "don't you use this house like a hotel", well I'm not being horrible but Laurens at that age where she was doing that. The only time I ever used to intervene with Lauren and her Mum was when Lauren used to tell Nik to "FUCK OFF" and I was like "WHOOOOOO STOP THAT NOW"! I used to tell her "you can row all day long but don't you ever tell your Mum to fuck off" I couldn't accept that. I know I wasn't her

Dad but it was my house she was living in and I paid the rent so I expected people to live by my rules, I don't ask for much with them rules just don't tell people to fuck off and tidy up after yourself.

I've said it so many times that if I could live on a desert island just me, Nik and the girls I'd love that. When it's just me and Nik we get on so well and that woman understands me more than anyone on this planet. I know a lot of my friends have split up with their girlfriends then they're living with another bird two months later, well that's not me and it never will be. I have trust issues with everybody because I don't trust anybody apart from Nik. The one thing I want Nik to be is to be happy and if she finds happiness with someone else then good luck to her. Only time will tell but I'm just so tired of us being in this position. I deserve to be happy in life as well as her. If and when Nik gets with another bloke other than me then that's when everything changes. The last bloke Nik was with before me was a two-bit drug dealer who used to beat her up so do you think I'm gonna let somebody like that around Bella? Anybody who's is going to be around my Daughter I'll be doing my homework on, as any man would. I just want her to be happy and as for me and Nik just being friends? Well I've got a million friends already! I wanna be with Nik, they'll never be anyone else for me but that woman.

Nik used to think when I was out working on the weekend with the boxing I was shagging the ring card girls, well nobody was interested in me because when I was at work I was a horrible cunt. I was there to protect people and was a strong-arm and that's all it ever was.

The biggest struggle I have in my life these days is with money. I struggle with the rent on a month to month basis and my young fighter Ben Jones is the same. I spoke to him the other day and I could tell there was something wrong. I asked him and he told me he was struggling to find his rent but I told him to fuck the money. Concentrate on your fight. Fuck the money I've got an overdraft facility I'll get it for you if needs be. That's why I go out of my way to help him with his ticket sales or sponsor money because I know what he's going through but we pull in together as a team.

I hope maybe the lord gives me another 30 years and I'm still here when I'm one of them old fuckers shitting and pissing the bed. Whoever reads this book I want them to realise the battle I have every day to do the right thing. I want people to realise the carrots that have been dangled in front of me. I want people like myself to persevere with the dark depression when some days you don't want to get out of bed. There's many days even now when I sit on the settee with the duvet and I'm fucking scared stiff some days. It's the Mikey Sayki's and Ben Jones' that make me get up on a morning. We're in this together and them boys give me back things in life that even to this day they've not got a Scooby-doo about.

Of course, in life and in boxing it's about the money but it's also about the loyalty and I'm the loyalist cunt out there. Nobody can compete with my loyalty because I'm so black & white. This might sound very conceited but I wish more people in the world were like me in that respect but everybody's different ain't they?

What winds me up is the people on Facebook who maybe give a tramp a couple of quid then share it to boost their egos. Well Dominic Negus does things like that everyday but that never gets a mention, I'm only ever known for the bad things like knocking bad cunts out. One girl that always stays in my mind was a very talented girl on Southend front and she's there most days playing the violin. Bella always says, "Dad can we give her some money" and we always slip her a fiver but it doesn't mean I put it on social media does it. I was in Liverpool quite recently and some guy who was obviously homeless was playing on his guitar, I said "do us a favour mate can you play me Here Comes the Sun by The Beatles, there's a tenner for your troubles". Well I was stood there listening to him almost in tears and he made my fucking day. In fact fuck it I'll admit it he made a big horrible bear like me cry because I'm very in touch with my music.

There's certain songs that remind me of things and as I've said earlier in the book when I heard that song before my I.D parade I knew I was going to be alright. I have to say my favourite song of all time is Love Don't Live Here Anymore by Jimmy Nail. Here Comes the Sun though has a special place in my heart. Mine and Nik's favourite song was Are You Ready for Love by Elton John from 2003.That was out at the time I was bang in trouble with the possible trial looming over me and my nut went so my friend took me away to Cambridge for a few days. The lyrics to that song are "just call my name and I'll be there" but I remember sitting feeling sorry for myself thinking I can't even be there for Nik can I?! Another song called Science of Silence by Richard Ashcroft is another outstanding song. That song actually saved my life and stopped me doing myself in. Sometimes I've heard musicians saying "Well I only wrote Wonderwall when I was stoned" I wish these fella's in the bands realised what music can do to people. Every time I ever listen to Science of Silence it strikes a really good cord in me even though it's a kind of down song it saved my life 100%.

I'm now on my new journey in this life away from the shit and into the light. All I want this book to do is to get it across that I wasn't a hard man and I wasted a lot of my potential by being an idiot. I could have done so much better with so many things and I'm not just talking about the fight game.

In 2018 particularly it really dawned on me just how stupid I've been in my life and how much loyalty I've shown towards people that don't deserve it because my loyalty is second to none. No-one can come near me on that and only in the last few weeks I've seen things from the people who were allegedly supposed to be close to me, but they've sold me down the road for a plate of food.

Unfortunately, when I was putting this book to bed there was a few things that happened and certain people have drifted away who I'd have fucking died for. From now on in 2019 and beyond that I have to do a lot more for myself and it's just me and Bella against the world. I've been so shit on and I know a lot of people who used to be around me until only a few weeks ago are expecting me to go back to the old Dom and start showing my teeth and growling but it's not happening. What's happened instead is that I've just gone really quiet and it's maybe made a couple of people nervous. To be quite truthful a couple of fighters I had have decided to part company with me but these are the same people I turned down jobs for stupid money for so that I could guide their careers. In the harsh light of reality they've done me a favour and it's made me realise I'm now 48 years old and I've got nothing because I've always looked after everybody else. Just like them three geezers who attacked me with an axe back in 2003 done me a favour then maybe the couple of lads who've pissed off have done me a massive fucking favour. It's just made me realise all the things I've done for people doesn't mean shit. All I ever wanted was a bit of loyalty and they couldn't do that so it doesn't matter now. Boxing is a dog eat dog world out there and there ain't no loyalty in boxing. Mickey Duff once said, "If you want loyalty get a dog" and he was so fucking right. He also told his fighter Lloyd Honeyghan "there's nothing in our contract that says we've got to like each other".

I'd like to think my old man would be proud of me because of my balls and my loyalty because that's how he brought me up. The reason I went so wonky in later years wasn't down to my Dad, that was me, purely me. We all want to be a somebody in life don't we? We don't want to end up just dust in a box and maybe for many years I was heading in the wrong direction in life. These days though what matters now is that when I meet the grim reaper that my little girl Annabella can say, "he wasn't a bad fella my old Dad, he was alright". That's my goal now, not to see how many people in one night I can knock out.

Now you've read 'Into the Light' please take this as an open apology to the people out there I hurt. Yes, I know many won't even read this because they'll have already said, "Ooh he's a fucking idiot" and believe me I've read many many things about me on social media usually from fake accounts. To them people I'd like to say I've paid my dues and I've learnt the hard way. I've took my licks (and axes) and I've deserved what I got. I've done bad but I would say sometimes in my life I've been so misunderstood by people who've just formed an opinion of me within the first couple of minutes.

I feel like I've been in rehab for the last 15 years since Bella was born and now I'm 48. I thought things would have been different, they should have been different, but it's down to me to change it. I'm not like everybody thinks I am. All I've ever wanted to be in life was loved, that's why and although I've never done it, I can relate to these football hooligans, come the weekend they were part of something like a family. Normally you find if you read these Carlton Leach and Cass Pennant books they got on with their gangs better than their own families and I can understand that.

Being bad doesn't interest me anymore… but I'm still the fucking man though! (laughs)

Ben Jones

My Brother and my Mum had always been onto me about joining a boxing club. Growing up I would watch it on TV in awe of fighters. I wasn't really concentrating at school, I was obviously pissing about so my Mum got my Brother to take me down the boxing gym when we moved to Chingford. I'd never heard of Dominic Negus at that point but my Brother knew of him. In fact, the only time I'd heard his name was when a group of lads were talking about him in the barbers one day with tales of what he used to get up to in Essex.

The first time I went in Dom's gym I was bunking off school when I was about fifteen and I just popped my head round for a nosey and I saw this big imposing bald-headed geezer shouting "Hello son, come in then I won't hurt you". I kind of shuffled in because when you meet Dom for the first time you think 'oh fucking hell' but once you really get to know him he's a big friendly giant. From the day I met Dom, even though I never had one amateur fight I stayed in his gym and I signed pro forms the week before my 18th birthday. I trained for the full three years to get ready for the professional ranks because I was never suited to the unpaid code. From 6am I was there every day with Dom then from 2pm – 9pm I worked there so we kind of have never left each other's side.

I had a few unlicensed fights when I was sixteen and sort of cleared up in my area but there wasn't really much competition for somebody like me who wanted to make a living from boxing so Dom spoke to Frank Warren's right-hand man Andy Ayling to come and have a look at me fighting and I got a contract with Frank Warren. Dominic is really like a father figure to me because in my life although I'm blessed with an angel of a Mum my dad was a proper bastard. Dom's almost filled that role to me. Dom took me to restaurants and from the day I met him everywhere he's went I've went.

Dom looks out for me far more than just with the boxing. One incident when Dom took me over to Spain for sparring we entered a restaurant, now anyone who knows me knows I'm not a rude person but there was this singer in there being abusive to me and even at one point said he was going to cut me. Well Dom shouted "PARDON" of course you can imagine what happened next but that was the first and last time I've ever seen Dom put it on someone. He didn't do anything psychically but Dom went from 0 to 100 within seconds and I'd never seen him like that before. Dominic has got my back and he wouldn't let anybody bad mouth me. Another time after I'd boxed I had my girlfriend and a few of her friends talking to me around the ring and they were all good-looking girls. Well I didn't see it but there was another couple of guys just on the corner of the ring who didn't like me talking to the good-looking girls. So, these lads started getting rowdy and looking for trouble but straight away Dominic went over and took all three blokes out of the area away from me. Dominic told them all to fuck off and off they went.

Only last week me and Dom were on the way to the gym and we went past this guy from our area, I won't mention his name but he's been stealing money from Dom's partner Ian and a few others. Well this guy is known for being a right rat and Dominic hadn't seen him for a while. In fact. Dom didn't click on who it was it was only when I said that was that fella who's had Ian over, well I've never seen Dominic move so fast and when he caught up with the fella with the rats face just dropped! He knew he was fucked and he had an angry Dominic Negus in front of him. Well the guy was telling Dominic how sorry he was and how he'd changed even though he'd been ripping people off left, right and centre in Essex. Dominic kind of half- heartedly nutted him and told him he should be ashamed of himself because Ian had been so good to the guy who's just blatantly taken the piss. If you've seen the film Rock 'n' Rolla and the bit where he goes "don't hit me Archie I'm only little", god it was so funny but not for the robbing rat.

Now me and Mikey are always winding Dom up about saying "don't hit me Dom I'm only little"! (laughs)

I've just recently passed my driving test so I'm still learning but I had a really funny incident with Dom in my car only about five months ago. Well I was sort of at fault and I went past this lorry when I shouldn't have. Well the driver was mega pissed off and he pulled over to my side shouting "DO YOU FUCKING LIKE YOUR CAR MATE?" obviously in a threatening manner because he could only see me. The next thing Dom's stuck his head out of the window telling him to calm down and acknowledged I'd messed up. Well the bloke kept on effing and blinding so Dominic's lost his temper and shouted back "What ya wanna do about it then ya cunt"???? but the blokes kept telling Dom to fuck off, well it didn't happen how you'd expect and the next thing was Dominic's just started laughing in his face and he surprised me with that one. I think that's the only time I've ever known him to start laughing in that western kind of standoff situation. Dom was the bigger man on that one I'll give him that. To the man in that lorry you were definitely blessed by the gods above on that day.

I'm only twenty-one now and basically I'm planning on having another ten years in the game. Whatever Dominic Negus says I'll believe him. I'm thankful I've only ever had him in my life regarding the boxing and I'm happy with him. Me and my gym mate Mikey Sakyi have full confidence in Dominic and even if its problems away from boxing we both go to Dominic for advice. If I have women problems I'll go to Dominic. I love the big fucker and you couldn't describe that man in only a couple of sentences. Dom's just a legend.

After my second pro fight Dom promised me if I won he'd take me to see my all-time hero Ricky Hatton. For me growing up Ricky was the man and still today he's my favourite fighter in the history of the sport. So, I've won the fight and true to his word Dom took me up to Manchester and as soon as I walked in I was like 'OH MY FUCKING GOD' I was star struck. It was like being in Madam Tussauds but obviously better. Well when I met Ricky he was just sitting there taking the piss out of me constantly. Ricky Hatton is one of them people you meet and he's exactly like you'd want your idol to be.

I've been in the ring when it's not been going right. It's funny because when I was still on the unlicensed scene I had Dom in my corner and at one point I was crying I swear to god but Dom was there for me and I listened to his advice and got through it. He's not a bad bloke to have in your corner and just in life in general is he? When I'm about to box he gets in the ring with me and he's by my side until we touch gloves and that's a big thing because some fighters just let their fighters go in there on their own. Dom tells me when I go into battle he's as close to me right until the last second and that's just what he's like to me with everything in life.

I love you Dom ya big fucker X.

Mike Jackson
Ricky Hatton's Assistant Trainer

Before I met Dominic Negus I was aware of him because he was a good boxer winning the Southern Area title. At the same time I was hearing about the other things that Dominic was getting up to out of the ring, I'd heard that he could be a little bit naughty.

For me, with Dominic, I can only speak as I find and I find him to be a lovely bloke. What a lot of people don't realise about Dominic is that he was a nice boxer in the amateurs but when Dominic saw the red mist, all of that went out of the window, he'd lose his cool and become a bit of a liability. Dominic beat some of the top names in the amateurs at the time, like Billy Bessey for example so that proves that his boxing skill was very underestimated.

I didn't actually meet Dominic personally until the early 2000's when Dominic was usually working as security on Frank Warrens shows. It's funny because the first time I met him, Dominic knew the fella I work with, Brian Hughes from Collyhurst, he knew him and you can have a laugh with Dom, even though Dominic is twice the size of me I could always have banter with him. I'd look over at him and I'd say to him "what you looking at" and he'd say "I'm looking at you, you northern slag" and I'd say to him "I'll take you outside in a minute" knowing full well that he could wipe the floor with me but we always had that kind of banter and we got on with each other from day one.

I was always comfortable with Dom, even though I knew about some of his antics out of the ring, I always show people the respect that they show me and if people want to have a laugh and a joke with you then all the better. I speak as I find but I wouldn't believe he was the same person as the man I had heard the wild stories of. I've read his first book 'Out of the Shadows' and I wouldn't believe it was the same person.

One funny story is, when he first met my Wife Lynnette and we went out for a meal in Manchester, he gave her a big hug, he'd never set eyes on her before but I said to my Wife that she'd have to read his book, but Dom said "don't do that you might judge me" and my Wife looked at him in the eyes and said "what makes you think I haven't judged you already" and he said "fair play I'm having that" and them two just hit it off, my Wife is now a big fan of his, Dom's that kind of person. All Dom wants from people in life is for people to treat him as he treats them and I'm the same. I've never seen Dominic heavy handed but obviously at weigh ins around big fights I've seen him when he's had to be stern and he's had to drag people out of the way. I've never seen him take people down dark alleys and give them a kicking like people say he has. What you've got to understand is Dominic's so well respected throughout the fight game that no one in their right mind is going to really start on him in the first place. Dominic was hired to always look after the elite fighters because he was trusted and was the best at what he did.

When Dominic started training his lads, he invited me down to Chigwell in Essex to work the corner for Mike Sakyi and Boy Jones. Dominic at the time had a sore hip so I did the cuts and the corner but there are not many trainers that would ask another coach from another part of the country into the camp. That to me just shows that Dominic Negus doesn't have any ego and only wants the best for his lads. I even did the corner for Mike Sakyi on the big PPV show in Leeds when Josh Warrington won his world title.

The only negative thing I can say about Dominic is that he never answers his phone but that is very much down to his past. Dominic said he never answers calls after 9pm as that was the bewitching hour when the underworld would come alive.

I'd like to wish Dominic all the very best, me and my Wife Lynnette think the world of him and if there was ever anything he needed we would be right there for him.

Micky Theo

Actor/Doorman/Former MR Universe Contestant/ Lenny McLean's Best Friend

I first heard the name Dominic Negus long before I met him from when I was doing the doors in and around Essex. All of it I must say for fighting related things as he was climbing the ladder coming through as a young man doing naughty things.

I wouldn't meet Dom until the back end of the 90s when I just lost my best friend Lenny McLean. I used to train with Lenny and we did everything together and he sure was aware too of some kid called Negus going out and fighting in the clubs around London.

In the last couple of years me and Dom have really got to know each other well and started having breakfast together more frequently. You wouldn't know it to look at him but Dominic is a very funny guy and every time I've been in his company he has great humour.

Towards the time Dominic fought Audley Harrison in 2002 was when I'd say you couldn't fail to hear Dom's name around our little part of the woods for the various things he was up to. Yes, Dom was known in Essex for many of the wrong reasons but I never ever heard his name mixed in with the same sentence as taking liberties with people, definitely not.

Dominic likes a laugh and a joke but is very much a quiet guy as in he's never been out and looked for trouble. Dominic respects people but then people have tried in the past to take his kindness for a weakness and they've said the wrong things, then that's when you hear of the crazy Dominic Negus coming out to play.

It's only the bad people in life that ever had anything to worry about from Dominic Negus because all Dom wants to do is love everyone.

These days, certainly in the last few years Dom's seriously changed his life and become a better person in the sense that he's no longer working on doors. Dominic is no longer in that troubled aura where he had to have that attitude around him.

Back when Dominic was working the doors yes he had a huge name, so when a few lads went in one of his establishments and they played up he had to react just like my pal Lenny did when he was on the door. Lenny didn't like fighting but he did it to put food on the table and Dominic was the same. What you've got to remember is if Dominic didn't react to these young up and comers then it would go around that Dom was losing his touch or getting soft.

In your normal world if somebody said something out of order then you could just think he's pissed just ignore them, but on the doors we can't do that because myself and the likes of Dominic must defend our name our brand if you like. When Dominic was on them doors he had every mad bastard coming to try him out and he had to let everybody know, so it would spread like the great fire of London that nobody could fuck with him and that's what he did. You have to build a name up in the clubs over time, that's how it works and that's just what Dom did.

Don't forget you work alongside maybe another few faces on the door so if you let somebody take the piss out of you and insult you, your team watch and even spread it around. Then the next thing is "ooh I seen Negus the other week losing his touch and he's not the man he once was".

I'm there for Dominic and vice-versa but this morning I was talking to Dom over breakfast and he was telling me about how he was going to get his S.I.A badge back to do the doors a few nights a week. I told him that wouldn't be such a great idea to get back into the same shit, he's come out of that and I do hope he takes my advice. He's got a little girl to put first and I do know that if it wasn't for his little daughter he'd have been banged up a long time ago so I think he needs to concentrate on her because believe me she does keep him inline. Dom very much thinks of Bella before he steps out of line though so please Dom give that one a miss eh. Every time I've ever given Dominic advice he's always thankful and I know he listens.

I would say Dominic is 100% finished with his old life. I don't think he'd allow himself to even go there although anything in life is tempting isn't it? It just depends on how far you wanna go! I mean if you said to your average law-biding citizen to take X amount of money down the road in the boot of their car most of them would do it if you put enough money under their noses. Most of the straight people I know would be happy to earn 3-4 grand for one nights work believe me, but it's the exceptionally clever ones who think, hang on a minute, if I do that and I get caught I'm going away for ten years in Wormwood Scrubs. That amount of time for what? 3-4 grand? 10 grand? 20 grand? I don't fucking think so.

The Dominic Negus I know so well is the same as me and we've both never had anything to do with drugs. Yes I've had some of my friends doing well over the years making big money but their doing big time as well over it so you've got to ask yourself is it really worth it! It's only the fucking idiots who do them things and drive around with big cars and even the ones who seem to do well their only sat on a time bomb and they always get caught in the end.

I wouldn't say the word around Essex is Dom's settled down. Him as a person and a stand-up guy doesn't need to prove anything to the world. People know he's a handful so don't fuck about with him. I don't think any of us want to announce it, we become that way in life by going what we've gone through. Just because Dominic Negus can't be arsed with all that shit anymore doesn't mean he's not still capable or that you could go take liberties with the man. Even a Lion who is the king of the jungle has to every now and again go around and fuck shit up and maybe bite a few jackals to keep the young cubs in line. That's very much Dominic Negus. Only this morning Dominic was telling me he's back on the tools and out on the sites working on the digger which I'm so happy to hear. That man will do anything for work as long as it doesn't risk a custodial sentence and that's how it should be.

My personal message for Dominic is to keep his head down, be strong and think of his daughter. Always think before you take the next step and then you'll do the right thing and you'll be ahead of everyone. Love ya Dom. Your friend Micky Theo X

Iain McCallister

Boss at Man Commercial Security

I worked with Dominic many, many years ago when he used to work for Top Guard which was a rival security company nearly 20 years ago now. Dominic Negus is very good with his mouth so he can defuse a situation just as good as anything he can do physically. In all the time I worked alongside him he certainly wasn't a bully. Yes, he can look after himself but he also demands respect from people not just because of his size but his demeanour. He doesn't go around chinning people for nothing like some people think he does, I mean I've seen him in situations where people have been screaming at him but he's never bitten because he's comfortable in his own skin and he knows he could finish people in a heartbeat if required.

Dom's a tough lad inside and outside of the ring but he prefers people to like him. I know Dominic very well and he'd hate for people to think of him as a bully because that's just so far removed from what he's actually about. I'd say he's more interested in going around trying to wind people up by being a practical joker because he's got a fabulous sense of humour.

What I'd say about Dom is that he's a great friend but he'd be a terrible enemy. I've done security for the big Frank Warren shows all over England, Ireland and Scotland alongside of Dom and no matter what city we're at somebody comes up and knows who Dominic is but he's always good and never once does he fail to have time for people.

I've always found that however misplaced Dominic Negus to be in life, I've found that his hearts been in the right place and not only that but whenever I did put on the security for the boxing PPV fights I found the fighters not only knew Dom but had a mutual respect because their paths have crossed as well. The Brighton Rock and former W.B.O title challenger Scott Welch always highly rated Dom's boxing ability so that must count for something mustn't it.

The overall opinion of Dominic going into the unlicensed scene was that he was too good for everybody in it. As far as work went I never had a problem putting Dom in charge of a world superstar like Bernard Hopkins or just down at The York Hall in Bethnal Green looking after some journeyman fighter the man has just no side to him.

There's very few people about in life that are as popular as him. Of course there's those that have done better in life than him but not everyone likes them. Dominic Negus has been blessed with one of them popular bubbly personality's big time.

Dominic Shepherd

My name is Dominic 'Jack' Shepherd and I'm 50 years old. I am the founder of Peacock White Collar Boxing. I had 30 bouts on the White-Collar circuit and have been promoting White Collar events operating out of The Peacock Gym in Canning Town in East London since 2002.

Spending most of my life living in and around the Essex area it was hard not to hear the name Dominic Negus. I first heard his name in my twenties when I was going to pubs and clubs when Dom was getting himself a reputation for being involved in serious aggravation.

I'm also a keen boxing fan so also knew of The Milky Bar Kid in his early pro days.

I spent a lot of time avoiding the man and if he was in my local bar in Buckhurst Hill I would spot him and go elsewhere.

I didn't know him and didn't want to know him either.

I remember ringing a club owner friend of mine one Saturday morning and saying,' Hi it's Dom' down the phone to him and he said, 'for fucks sake Dom what was all that about last night?' . When he realised it was me he asked me to go down to the club and when I went in he showed me the carnage from the night before that Dom was involved in. Even more reason now for me to avoid him.

Having the same first name there were many times over the years when I'd meet people and they'd say, 'Oh so you're Dominic, I've heard a lot about you' and I'd say, 'I'm not Dominic Negus I'm the Dominic who can't fight'.

There was a time when a friend of mine rang me from Kent and told me a story about the legendary fight figure the late Roy Shaw having road rage with a doorman and he had chinned him. They'd heard that the fella was a mate of Dominic's and I got the phone call. This guy went on and on saying that I needed to stop the man from going to the Police and that Roy wanted to see me. I interrupted him as fast as I could to tell him he'd got the wrong Dom. I met Roy a few years after that and he was a nice man but I didn't need to be put in the middle of that situation!!

I started promoting shows in 2002 and Dom was involved in the security of them.

One night I went to an audience with Roberto Duran and as I walked to the toilet I heard a booming voice say, 'Mr Shepherd'. I turned and it was Dominic Negus. I thought oh shit what have I done, I didn't even think he knew me. Dom invited me on to his table and we talked and talked for ages like old friends. I thought to myself he's a really good man and if I'm honest I regretted making a decision about him before we'd met. Since that evening we've been very close, talking or texting on a daily basis.

Through Dom's involvement with Sparta Gym in Chingford he has put a lot of boxers on my shows and I'm in there a lot watching sparring. Last summer I went in there in a pair of shorts and Dom asked me to bring in two coffees from the café next door. As I walked in being careful not to spill any of the drinks Dom crept up behind me and pulled my shorts and pants down in front of everyone in there. I'm still having nightmares over it. Even now if I visit my local supermarket and if I'm wearing shorts I always check to see that they are done up properly in case the big fella might be lurking in one of the aisles.

Whenever I walk in to Sparta I always get a volley of abuse from Dom and it really wouldn't be the same if that didn't happen.

Knowing the man how I do now Dom is really sensitive and very misunderstood. He is a very loyal man, he gives loyalty and expects it in return.

If you are close to him, honest and loyal then you really couldn't ask for a better friend. If you're not then you'd better still keep your wits about you....

Thanks

There's so many people I'd like to thank in this book.

Albie Turner and Peter Fares who sponsor my boys Ben and Mikey. I'd be fucked without their help.

My best friends ever Brynn Robinson and Henry Smith. Them two men more than saved my life on a dozen occasions and that ain't no bullshit. Them two are my family without being family.

My daughter Bella, without her my life would have been done a long time ago. I'd be in a graveyard or doing a life sentence.

Micky Theo and Bobby Wilcox have both stood by me when they didn't have to. Them two made a public stand for me when everyone in the world hated me. Both know I'm a good person.

Ian Wilson and all the people in the gym at Sparta.

Andy Horner-Glister and Barry Sanders are another two gents who deserve a mention who've sponsored Boy Jones Junior from day one because they see the potential in him.

Nik's Mum Lorraine and her partner John, oh my god I'd be lost without them.

John Kershaw was my angel and stuck by me when my nut was completely gone. He told me "don't worry Dom we're gonna get through this".

Andy Ayling deserves a mention for the help he's given me and the lads over the years.

Matt and Ben who I live with and who have to put up with such a horrible cunt like myself.

Also, for Audley Harrison, you can fuck off... Nah just kidding I totally respect Audley and I think he was a great fighter.

What are you expecting me to list a load of bad boy crime figures? Do me a favour Ha Ha....

Last but not least thank you to Nik for being there and for giving me the most amazing little girl in the world. You're not too bad yourself Nik X

Message from Dominic

If anyone wants to sponsor any of my lad's then please get in touch with me on Facebook via Dominic Anthony Negus. I have to use my full name on Facebook because some crazy cunt keeps making fake profiles of me and he keeps messaging people pretending to be me. It's a crazy world out there for sure!!!!

Also, if there's any young fighters out there wanting to go pro and need an old head like me to guide them then of course I'm happy to chat with them regardless of levels.